The W

Spee**ches**

The World's
greatest
Speeches

Compiled by
Vijaya Kumar

NEW DAWN PRESS, INC.
USA• UK• INDIA

NEW DAWN PRESS GROUP

Published by New Dawn Press Group

New Dawn Press, Inc., 244 South Randall Rd # 90, Elgin, IL 60123
e-mail: sales@newdawnpress.com

New Dawn Press, 2 Tintern Close, Slough, Berkshire, SL1-2TB, UK
e-mail: sterlingdis@yahoo.co.uk

New Dawn Press (An Imprint of Sterling Publishers (P) Ltd.)
A-59, Okhla Industrial Area, Phase-II, New Delhi-110020
e-mail: sterlingpublishers@airtelbroadband.in
www.sterlingpublishers.com

The World's Greatest Speeches
© 2006, Sterling Publishers Pvt. Ltd.
ISBN 1-84557-608-X

PRINTED IN INDIA

CONTENTS

PREFACE

Speeches have their origin in antiquity. As civilisations progressed, speech-making started gaining importance. By the time civilisation flourished in Greece, eloquence of speech and oratory became a valuable tool of government and culture. It continues to be a powerful medium of communication with the masses.

This volume is a collection of the most famous and the most inspiring addresses by great personalities like Swami Vivekananda, Martin Luther King, George Washington, Mahatma Gandhi, Nelson Mandela, Napolean Bonaparte, Garibaldi Giuseppe, Mikhail Gorbachev, Karl Marx, Franklin Roosevelt, Harry S Truman, John Kennedy, Winston Churchill, and so on. Care has been exercised to include not merely the famous masterpieces of eloquence, but also the great historic addresses which have left their footprints on the sands of time with their powerful thought and logical presentation.

While some are fiery and impassioned speeches, others are learned, philosophical, or reflective, satirical or humourous. These speeches will inspire readers and provide public speakers with ideas for powerful openings, effective transitions, impressive endings, provocative themes, historic parallels, and memorable quotations.

1. CLEMENT R ATTLEE (1946–)

Clement Richard Attlee was the Labour prime minister of Britain from 1945 to 1951. He gave the following speech on 29 October 1941 at the ILO conference.

We do not envisage an end to this victory. We are determined not only to win the war but to win peace. Plans must be prepared in advance. Action must be taken now if the end of the war is not to find us unprepared. But the problems of peace cannot be solved by one nation in isolation. The plans of a postwar Britain must be fitted into the plans of a postwar world, for this fight is not just a fight between nations. It is a fight for the future civilisation. Its results will affect the lives of all men and women — not only those now engaged in the struggle.

It is certain that until the crushing burden of armaments throughout the world is lifted from the back of the people, they cannot enjoy the maximum social being which is possible. We cannot build the city of our desire under the constant menace of aggression. Freedom from fear and freedom from want must be sought together.

The joint expression of aims common to the United States and the British Commonwealth of Nations known as the Atlantic Charter includes not only purposes covering war but outlines of more distant objectives.

It binds us to endeavour with due respect to our existing obligations to further the enjoyment by all states — great and small.

Britain gives thanks to those statesmen who, in spite of the immensity of their problems, have given months of their efforts to assure the maintenance of a peace which the demands of Italy disturb.

The Ethiopian Government, the Ethiopian church and all her people pray to God that He may assist and direct them in their efforts for the maintenance of peace. Ethiopia is conscious of having always fulfilled all her international obligations and having until now made all the sacrifices compatible with her honour and dignity to assure a peaceful solution of the present conflict.

Britain wishes and hopes with all her heart that an amicable and peaceful settlement, in accordance with right and justice, will intervene, and the officers of the Council of the League of Nations, in conformity with the pact, will compel all the nations of the world, great and small, who hold a peace as their ideal to halt this crisis which threatens to stop all civilisation.

2. TONY BLAIR (1953–)

Anthony Charles Lyndon Blair is the prime minister of United Kingdom, First Lord of the Treasury, and Minister for the Civil Service.

The following is the speech on the London bombings, delivered at the Labour Party national conference in August 2005.

The greatest danger is that we fail to face up to the nature of the threat we are dealing with. What we witnessed in London last Thursday week was not an aberrant act. It was not random. It was not a product of particular local circumstances in West Yorkshire.

Senseless though any such horrible murder is, it was not without sense for its organisers. It had a purpose. It was done according to a plan it was meant. What we are confronting here is an evil ideology. It is not a clash of civilisations — all civilised people, Muslim or others, feel revulsion at it. But it is a global struggle and it is a battle of ideas, hearts and minds, both within Islam and outside it. This is the battle that must be won, a battle not just about the terrorist methods but their views. Not just their barbaric acts, but their barbaric ideas. Not only what they do but what they think and the thinking they would impose on others.

This ideology and the violence that is inherent in it did not start a few years ago in response to a particular policy. Over the past 12 years, al-Qaeda and its associates have attacked 26 countries, killed thousands of people, many of them Muslims. They have networks in virtually every major country and thousands of fellow travellers. They are well-financed. Look at their websites. They aren't unsophisticated in their propaganda. They recruit however and whoever they can and with success. Neither is it true that they have no demands. They do. It is just that no sane person would negotiate on them.

This is a religious ideology.... . Those who kill in its name believe genuinely that in doing it, they do God's work; they go to paradise. They demand the elimination of Israel; the withdrawal of all Westerners from Muslim countries, irrespective of the wishes of people and government; the establishment of effectively Taliban states and Sharia law in the Arab world en route to one caliphate of all Muslim nations.

We don't have to wonder what type of country those states would be. Afghanistan was such a state. Girls put out of school. Women denied even rudimentary rights. People living in abject poverty and oppression. All of it justified by reference to religious faith.

The twentieth century showed how powerful political ideologies could be. This is a religious ideology, a strain within the worldwide religion of Islam, as far removed from its essential decency and truth as Protestant gunmen who kill Catholics, or vice versa, are from Christianity. But do not let us underestimate it or dismiss it. Those who kill in its name believe genuinely that in doing it, they do God's work; they go to paradise.

From the mid-1990s onwards, statements from al-Qaeda, gave very clear expression to this ideology: "Every Muslim, the minute he can start differentiating, carries hatred towards the Americans, Jews and Christians. This is part of our ideology. The creation of Israel is a crime and it has to be erased.

You should know that targeting Americans and Jews and killing them anywhere you find them on the earth is one of the greatest duties and one of the best acts of piety you can offer to God Almighty. Just as great is their hatred for so-called apostate governments in Muslim countries. This is why mainstream Muslims are also regarded as legitimate targets.

At last year's (Labour) party conference, I talked about this ideology in these terms. Its roots are not superficial, but deep, in the madrassas of Pakistan, in the extreme forms of Wahabi doctrine in Saudi Arabia, in the former training camps of al-Qaeda in Afghanistan; in the cauldron of Chechnya; in parts of the politics of most countries of the Middle East and many in Asia; in the extremist minority that now in every European city preach hatred of the West and our way of life. This is what we are up against. It cannot be beaten except by confronting it, symptoms and causes, head-on. Without compromise and without delusion.

The extremist propaganda is cleverly aimed at their target audience. It plays on our tolerance and good nature. It exploits the tendency to guilt of the developed world — as if it is our behaviour that should change, that if we only tried to work out and act on their grievances, we could lift this evil, that if we changed our behaviour, they would change theirs. This is a misunderstanding of a catastrophic order. Their cause is not founded on an injustice. It is founded on a belief, one whose fanaticism is such it can't be moderated. It can't be remedied. It has to be stood up to. And, of course, they will use any issue that is a matter of dissent within our democracy. But we should lay bare the almost-devilish logic behind such manipulation.

If it is the plight of the Palestinians that drives them, why, every time it looks as if Israel and Palestine are making progress, does the same ideology perpetrate an outrage that turns hope back into despair? If it is Afghanistan that motivates them, why blow up innocent Afghans on their way to their first ever election? If it is Iraq that motivates them, why is the same ideology killing Iraqis by terror in defiance of an elected Iraqi government?

What was September 11, 2001 the reprisal for? Why even after the first Madrid bomb (in March 2004) and the election of a new Spanish government were they planning another atrocity when caught? In the end, it is by the power of argument, debate, true religious faith and true legitimate politics that we will defeat this threat. Why, if it is the cause of Muslims that concerns them, do they kill so many with such callous indifference? We must pull this up by its roots. Within Britain, we must join up with our Muslim community to take on the extremists. Worldwide, we should confront it everywhere it exists.

Next week I and other party leaders will meet key members of the Muslim community. Out of it I hope we can get agreed action to take this common fight forward. I want also to work with other nations to promote the true face of Islam worldwide. Round the world, there are conferences already being held, numerous interfaith dialogues in place, but we need to bring all of these activities together and give them focus.

We must be clear about how we win this struggle. We should take what security measures we can. But let us not kid ourselves. In the end, it is by the power of argument, debate, true religious faith and true legitimate politics that we will defeat this threat.

That means not just arguing against their terrorism, but their politics and their perversion of religious faith. It means exposing as the rubbish it is, the propaganda about America and its allies wanting to punish Muslims or eradicate Islám. It means championing our values of freedom, tolerance and respect for others. It means explaining why the suppression of women and the disdain for democracy are wrong.

The idea that elected governments are the preserve of those of any other faith or culture, is insulting and wrong. Muslims believe in democracy just as much as any other faith and, given the chance, show it. We must step up the urgency of our efforts. Here and abroad, the times the terrorists have succeeded are all too well known. Less known are the times they have been foiled. The human life destroyed we can see. The billions of dollars every nation now spends is huge and growing. And they kill without limit. They murdered over 50 innocent people (in London last week. But it could have been over 500. And had it been, they would have rejoiced.

The spirit of our age is one in which the prejudices of the past are put behind us, where our diversity is our strength. It is this which is under attack. Moderates are not moderate through weakness but through strength. Now is the time to show it in defence of our common values.

3. EDMUND BURKE (1729–1797)

Edmund Burke was a British parliamentarian, a political philosopher and an orator.

The following is a speech that he delivered in the House of Commons in 1783.

*D*espite the act of 1773, there were still concerns about the administration of India.... . Our conquest there, after twenty years, is as crude as it was the first day. The natives scarcely know what it is to see the grey head of an Englishman. Young men (boys almost) govern there, without society, and without sympathy with the natives. They have no more social habits with the people, than if they still resided in England; nor, indeed, any species of intercourse but that which is necessary to making a sudden fortune, with a view to a remote settlement. Animated with all the avarice of age, and all the impetuosity of youth, they roll in one after another; wave after wave; and there is nothing before the eyes of the natives but an endless, hopeless prospect of new flights of birds of prey and passage, with appetites continually renewing for a food that is continually wasting. Every rupee of profit made by an Englishman is lost forever to India. With us are no retributory superstitions by which a foundation of charity compensates, through ages, to the poor, for the rapine and injustice of a day. With us no pride erects stately monuments which repair the mischiefs which pride had produced, and which adorn a country out of its own spoils. England has erected no churches, no hospitals, no palaces, no schools; England has built no bridges, made no high roads, cut no navigations, dug out no reservoirs. Every other conqueror of every other description has left some monument, either of state or beneficence, behind him. Were we to be driven out of India this day, nothing would remain, to tell that it had been possessed, during the inglorious period of our dominion, by anything better than the ourang-ourang or the tiger.

There is nothing in the boys we send to India worse than in the boys whom we are whipping at school, or that we see trailing a pike, or bending over a desk at home. But as English youth in India drink the intoxicating draught of authority and dominion before their heads are able to bear it, and as they are full grown in fortune long before they are ripe in principle, neither nature nor reason have any opportunity to exert themselves for remedy of the excesses of their premature power. The consequences of their conduct, which in good minds (and many of theirs are probably such) might produce penitence or amendment, are unable to pursue the rapidity of their flight. Their prey is lodged in England; and the cries of India are given to seas and winds, to be blown about, in every breaking up of the monsoon, over a remote and unhearing ocean.

In India all the vices operate by which sudden fortune is acquired; in England are often displayed, by the same persons, the virtues which dispense hereditary wealth. Arrived in England, the destroyers of the nobility and gentry of a whole kingdom will find the best company in this nation, at a board of elegance and hospitality. Here the manufacturer and husbandman will bless the just and punctual hand that in India has torn the cloth from the loom, or wrested the scanty portion of rice and salt from the peasant of Bengal, or wrung from him the very opium in which he forgot his oppressions and his oppressor. They marry into your families; they enter into your senate; they ease your estates by loans; they raise their value by demand; they cherish and protect your relations which lie heavy on your patronage; and there is scarcely a house in the kingdom that does not feel some concern and interest that makes all reform of our eastern government appear officious and disgusting; and, on the whole, a most discouraging attempt. In such an attempt you hurt those who are able to return kindness, or to resent injury. If you succeed, you save those who cannot so much as give you thanks. All these things show the difficulty of the work we have on hand; but they show its necessity too.

Our Indian government is in its best state, a grievance. It is necessary that the corrective should be uncommonly vigorous; and the work of men, sanguine, warm, and even impassioned in the cause. But it is an arduous thing to plead against abuses of a power which originates from your own country, and affects those whom we are used to consider as strangers.

4. GEORGE W BUSH (1946–)

George W Bush is serving a second term as the president of the United States of America.

On 11 September 2001 four large passenger jets were hijacked and piloted into the twin towers of the World Trade Center at New York and the Pentagon at Washington, killing over 3,000 persons. President Bush gave this much-anticipated speech before a joint session of Congress on 20 September 2001.

Mr Speaker, Mr President Pro Tempore, members of Congress, and fellow Americans:

In the normal course of events, presidents come to this chamber to report on the state of the Union. Tonight, no such report is needed. It has already been delivered by the American people.

We have seen it in the courage of passengers who rushed terrorists to save others on the ground. Passengers like an exceptional man named Todd Beamer. And would you please help me welcome his wife Lisa Beamer here tonight?

We have seen the state of our Union in the endurance of rescuers working past exhaustion.

We've seen the unfurling of flags, the lighting of candles, the giving of blood, the saying of prayers in English, Hebrew and Arabic.

We have seen the decency of a loving and giving people who have made the grief of strangers their own.

My fellow citizens, for the last nine days, the entire world has seen for itself the state of the Union, and it is strong.

Tonight, we are a country awakened to danger and called to defend freedom. Our grief has turned to anger and anger to resolution. Whether we bring our enemies to justice or bring justice to our enemies, justice will be done.

I thank the Congress for its leadership at such an important time.

All of America was touched on the evening of the tragedy to see Republicans and Democrats joined together on the steps of this Capitol singing "God Bless America".

And you did more than sing. You acted, by delivering $40 billion to rebuild our communities and meet the needs of our military. Speaker Hastert, Minority Leader Gephardt, Majority Leader Daschle and Senator Lott, I thank you for your friendship, for your leadership and for your service to our country.

And on behalf of the American people, I thank the world for its outpouring of support.

America will never forget the sounds of our national anthem playing at Buckingham Palace, on the streets of Paris and at Berlin's Brandenburg Gate.

We will not forget South Korean children gathering to pray outside our embassy in Seoul, or the prayers of sympathy offered at a mosque in Cairo.

We will not forget moments of silence and days of mourning in Australia and Africa and Latin America.

Nor will we forget the citizens of 80 other nations who died with our own. Dozens of Pakistanis, more than 130 Israelis, more than 250 citizens of India, men and women from El Salvador, Iran, Mexico and Japan, and hundreds of British citizens.

America has no truer friend than Great Britain. Once again, we are joined together in a great cause. I'm so honoured the British prime minister has crossed an ocean to show his unity with America. Thank you for coming, friend.

On September the 11th, enemies of freedom committed an act of war against our country. Americans have known wars, but for the past 136 years they have been wars on foreign soil, except for one Sunday in 1941. Americans have known the casualties of war, but not at the center of a great city on a peaceful morning.

Americans have known surprise attacks, but never before on thousands of civilians.

All of this was brought upon us in a single day, and night fell on a different world, a world where freedom itself is under attack.

Americans have many questions tonight. Americans are asking, "Who attacked our country?"

The evidence we have gathered all point to a collection of loosely affiliated terrorist organisation known as al-Qaeda. They are some of the murderers indicted for bombing American embassies in Tanzania and Kenya and responsible for bombing the USS Cole. Al-Qaeda is to terror what the Mafia is to crime. But its goal is not making money. Its goal is remaking the world and imposing its radical beliefs on people everywhere. The terrorists practice a fringe form of Islamic extremism that has been rejected by Muslim scholars and the vast majority of Muslim clerics; a fringe movement that perverts the peaceful teachings of Islam. The terrorists' directive commands them to kill Christians and Jews, to kill all Americans and make no distinctions among military and civilians, including women and children.

This group and its leader, a person named Osama bin Laden, are linked to many other organizations in different countries, including the Egyptian Islamic Jihad, the Islamic Movement of Uzbekistan.

There are thousands of these terrorists in more than 60 countries. They are recruited from their own nations and neighbourhoods and brought to camps in places like Afghanistan, where they are trained in the tactics of terror. They are sent back to their homes or sent to hide in countries around the world to plot evil and destruction.

The leadership of al-Qaeda has great influence in Afghanistan and supports the Taliban regime in controlling most of that country. In Afghanistan we see al-Qaeda's vision for the world. It is not only repressing its own people, it is threatening people everywhere by sponsoring and sheltering and supplying terrorists. By aiding and abetting murder, the Taliban regime is committing murder. And tonight the United States of America makes the following demands on the Taliban.

Deliver to United States authorities all of the leaders of al-Qaeda who hide in your land. Release all foreign nationals, including American citizens you have unjustly imprisoned. Protect foreign journalists, diplomats and aid workers in your country. Close immediately and permanently every terrorist training camp in Afghanistan. And hand over every terrorist and every person and their support structure to appropriate authorities. Give the United States full access to terrorist training camps, so we can make sure they are no longer operating. These demands are not open to negotiation or discussion.

The Taliban must act and act immediately. They will hand over the terrorists, or they will share in their fate.

I also want to speak tonight directly to Muslims throughout the world. We respect your faith. It's practiced freely by many millions of Americans and by millions more in countries that America counts as friends. Its teachings are good and peaceful, and those who commit evil in the name of Allah blaspheme the name of Allah.

The terrorists are traitors to their own faith, trying, in effect, to hijack Islam itself.

The enemy of America is not our many Muslim friends. It is not our many Arab friends. Our enemy is a radical network of terrorists and every government that supports them.

Our war on terror begins with al-Qaeda, but it does not end there. It will not end until every terrorist group of global reach has been found, stopped and defeated.

Americans are asking, "How will we fight and win this war?" We will direct every resource at our command – every means of diplomacy, every tool of intelligence, every instrument of law enforcement, every financial influence and every necessary weapon of war – to the destruction and to the defeat of the global terror network.

Now this war will not be like the war against Iraq a decade ago, with a decisive liberation of territory and a swift conclusion. It will not look like the air war above Kosovo two years ago, where no ground troops were used and not a single American was lost in combat.

Our response involves far more than instant retaliation and isolated strikes. Americans should not expect one battle, but a lengthy campaign unlike any other we have ever seen. It may include dramatic strikes visible on TV and covert operations secret even in success.

We will starve terrorists of funding, turn them one against another, drive them from place to place until there is no refuge or no rest. And we will pursue nations that provide aid or safe haven to terrorism. Every nation in every region now has a decision to make: Either you are with us, or you are with the terrorists.

From this day forward, any nation that continues to harbor or support terrorism will be regarded by the United States as a hostile regime. Our nation has been put on notice, we're not immune from attack. We will take defensive measures against terrorism to protect Americans.

Today, dozens of federal departments and agencies, as well as state and local governments, have responsibilities affecting homeland security.

These efforts must be coordinated at the highest level. So tonight, I announce the creation of a Cabinet-level position reporting directly to me — the Office of Homeland Security.

And tonight, I also announce a distinguished American to lead this effort, to strengthen American security: a military veteran — an effective governor, a true patriot, a trusted friend, Pennsylvania's Tom Ridge. He will lead, oversee and coordinate a comprehensive national strategy to safeguard our country against terrorism and respond to any attacks that may come.

These measures are essential. The only way to defeat terrorism as a threat to our way of life is to stop it, eliminate it and destroy it where it grows. Many will be involved in this effort, from FBI agents to intelligence operatives, to the reservists we have called to active duty. All deserve our thanks, and all have our prayers.

And tonight a few miles from the damaged Pentagon, I have a message for our military: Be ready. I have called the armed forces to alert, and there is a reason. The hour is coming when America will act, and you will make us proud.

This is not, however, just America's fight. And what is at stake is not just America's freedom. This is the world's fight. This is civilization's fight. This is the fight of all who believe in progress and pluralism, tolerance and freedom.

We ask every nation to join us. We will ask and we will need the help of police forces, intelligence services and banking systems around the world. The United States is grateful that many nations and many international organizations have already responded with sympathy and with support — nations from Latin America to Asia, to Africa, to Europe, to the Islamic world.

Americans are asking, "What is expected of us?" I ask you to live your lives and hug your children. I know many citizens have fears tonight, and I ask you to be calm and resolute, even in the face of a continuing threat. I ask you to uphold the values of America and remember why so many have come here.

We're in a fight for our principles, and our first responsibility is to live by them. No one should be singled out for unfair treatment or unkind words because of their ethnic background or religious faith. I ask you to continue to support the victims of this tragedy with your contributions. The thousands of FBI agents who are now at work in this investigation may need your cooperation, and I ask you to give it. I ask for your patience with the delays and inconveniences that may accompany tighter security and for your patience in what will be a long struggle. I ask your continued participation and confidence in the American economy. Terrorists attacked a symbol of American prosperity; they did not touch its source.

America is successful because of the hard work and creativity and enterprise of our people. These were the true strengths of our economy before September 11, and they are our strengths today.

And finally, please continue praying for the victims of terror and their families, for those in uniform and for our great country. Prayer has comforted us in sorrow and will help strengthen us for the journey ahead.

Tonight I thank my fellow Americans for what you have already done and for what you will do.

And ladies and gentlemen of the Congress, I thank you, their representatives, for what you have already done and for what we will do together. Tonight we face new and sudden national challenges.

We will come together to improve air safety, to dramatically expand the number of air marshals on domestic flights and take new measures to prevent hijacking.

We will come together to promote stability and keep our airlines flying with direct assistance during this emergency. We will come together to give law enforcement the additional tools it needs to track down terror here at home.

We will come together to strengthen our intelligence capabilities, to know the plans of terrorists before they act and to find them before they strike. We will come together to take active steps that strengthen America's economy and put our people back to work.

Tonight, we welcome two leaders who embody the extraordinary spirit of all New Yorkers, Governor George Pataki and Mayor Rudolf Giuliani. As a symbol of America's resolve, my administration will work with Congress and these two leaders to show the world that we will rebuild New York City.

After all that has just passed, all the lives taken and all the possibilities and hopes that died with them, it is natural to wonder if America's future is one of fear. Some speak of an age of terror. I know there are struggles ahead and dangers to face. But this country will define our times, not be defined by them. As long as the United States of America is determined and strong, this will not be an age of terror. This will be an age of liberty here and across the world.

It is my hope that in the months and years ahead, life will return almost to normal. We'll go back to our lives and routines, and that is good. But our resolve must not pass. Each of us will remember what happened that day and to whom it happened. We will remember the moment the news came, where we were and what we were doing. Some will remember an image of a fire or story or rescue. Some will carry memories of a face and a voice gone forever.

I will not forget the wound to our country and those who inflicted it. I will not yield, I will not rest, I will not relent in waging this struggle for freedom and security for the American people.

Fellow citizens, we'll meet violence with patient justice, assured of the rightness of our cause and confident of the victories to come. In all that lies before us, may God grant us wisdom, and may He watch over the United States of America.

5. JAMES EARL CARTER (1924–)

Jimmy Carter was the American Democrat president from 1977 to 1981.

The following is the inaugural address delivered on 20 January 1977 after assuming office of the president.

For myself and for our nation, I want to thank my predecessor for all he has done to heal our land.

In this outward and physical ceremony, we attest once again to the inner and spiritual strength of our nation. As my high school teacher, Miss Julia Coleman, used to say: "We must adjust to changing times and still hold to unchanging principles."

Here before me is the *Bible* used in the inauguration of our first President, in 1789, and I have just taken the oath of office on the Bible my mother gave me a few years ago, opened to a timeless admonition from the ancient prophet Micah: "He hath showed thee, O man, what is good; and what doth the Lord require of thee, but to do justly, and to love mercy, and to walk humbly with thy God. (Micah 6:8)"

This inauguration ceremony marks a new beginning, a new dedication within our government, and a new spirit among us all. A president may sense and proclaim that new spirit, but only a people can provide it.

Two centuries ago our nation's birth was a milestone in the long quest for freedom, but the bold and brilliant dream which excited the founders of this nation still awaits its consummation. I have no new dream to set forth today, but rather urge a fresh faith in the old dream.

Ours was the first society openly to define itself in terms of both spirituality and of human liberty. It is that unique self-definition which has given us an exceptional appeal. But it also imposes on us a special obligation, to take on those moral duties which, when assumed, seem invariably to be in our own best interests.

You have given me a great responsibility—to stay close to you, to be worthy of you, and to exemplify what you are. Let us create together a new national spirit of unity and trust. Your strength can compensate for my weakness, and your wisdom can help to minimise my mistakes.

Let us learn together and laugh together and work together and pray together, confident that in the end we will triumph together in the right. The American dream endures. We must once again have full faith in our country—and in one another. I believe America can be better. We can be even stronger than before. Let our recent mistakes bring a resurgent commitment to the basic principles of our nation, for we know that if we despise our own government we have no future. We recall in special times, when we have stood briefly, but magnificently, united. In those times, no prize was beyond our grasp.

But we cannot dwell upon remembered glory. We cannot afford to drift. We reject the prospect of failure or mediocrity or an inferior quality of life for any person. Our government must at the same time be both competent and compassionate.

We have already found a high degree of personal liberty, and we are now struggling to enhance equality of opportunity. Our commitment to human rights must be absolute, our laws fair, our natural beauty preserved; the powerful must not persecute the weak, and human dignity must be enhanced. We have learned that "more" is not necessarily "better," that even our great nation has its recognized limits, and that we can neither answer all questions nor solve all problems. We cannot afford to do everything, nor can we afford to lack boldness as we meet the future. So, together, in a spirit of individual sacrifice for the common good, we must simply do our best. Our nation can be strong abroad only if it is strong at home. And we know that the best way to enhance freedom in other lands is to demonstrate here that our democratic system is worthy of emulation.

To be true to ourselves, we must be true to others. We will not behave in foreign places so as to violate our rules and standards here at home, for we know that the trust which our nation earns is essential to our strength. The world itself is now dominated by a new spirit. People more numerous and more politically aware

are craving and now demanding their place in the sun—not just for the benefit of their own physical condition, but for basic human rights.

The passion for freedom is on the rise. Tapping this new spirit, there can be no nobler nor more ambitious task for America to undertake on this day of a new beginning than to help shape a just and peaceful world that is truly humane.

We are a strong nation, and we will maintain strength so sufficient that it need not be proven in combat—a quiet strength based not merely on the size of an arsenal, but on the nobility of ideas. We will be ever vigilant and never vulnerable, and we will fight our wars against poverty, ignorance, and injustice, for those are the enemies against which our forces can be honorably marshaled. We are a purely idealistic nation, but let no one confuse our idealism with weakness. Because we are free we can never be indifferent to the fate of freedom elsewhere. Our moral sense dictates a clearcut preference for these societies which share with us an abiding respect for individual human rights. We do not seek to intimidate, but it is clear that a world which others can dominate with impunity would be inhospitable to decency and a threat to the well-being of all people.

The world is still engaged in a massive armaments race designed to ensure continuing equivalent strength among potential adversaries. We pledge perseverance and wisdom in our efforts to limit the world's armaments to those necessary for each nation's own domestic safety. And we will move this year a step toward the ultimate goal—the elimination of all nuclear weapons from this earth. We urge all other people to join us, for success can mean life instead of death. Within us, the people of the United States, there is evident a serious and purposeful rekindling of confidence.

And I join in the hope that when my time as your president has ended, people might say this about our nation: that we had remembered the words of Micah and renewed our search for humility, mercy, and justice; that we had torn down the barriers that separated those of different race and region and religion, and where there had been mistrust, built unity, with a respect for diversity; that we had found productive work for those able to perform it; that we had strengthened the American family, which is the basis of our society; that we had ensured respect for the law, and equal treatment under the law, for the weak and the powerful, for the rich and the poor; and that we had enabled our people to be proud of their own government once again.

I would hope that the nations of the world might say that we had built a lasting peace, built not on weapons of war but on international policies which reflect our own most precious values.

These are not just my goals, and they will not be my accomplishments, but the affirmation of our nation's continuing moral strength.

6. NEVILLE CHAMBERLAIN (1869–1940)

Neville Chamberlain, an English statesman, was the prime minister of Britain from 1937 to 1940.

He gave this speech to the House of Commons on 1 September 1939, just when Hitler's troops had invaded Poland.

I do not propose to say many words tonight. The time has come when action rather than speech is required. Eighteen months ago, in this House I prayed that the responsibility might not fall upon me to ask this country to accept the awful arbitrament of war. I fear that I may not be able to avoid that responsibility.

But, at any rate, I cannot wish for conditions in which such a burden should fall upon me in which I should feel clearer than I do today as to where my duty lies.

No man can say that the Government could have done more to try to keep open the way for an honourable and equitable settlement of the dispute between Germany and Poland. Nor have we neglected any means of making it crystal clear to the German Government that if they insisted on using force again in the manner in which they had used it in the past, we were resolved to oppose them by force.

Now that all the relevant documents are being made public, we shall stand at the bar of history knowing that the responsibility for this terrible catastrophe lies on the shoulders of one man, the German Chancellor, who has not hesitated to plunge the world into misery in order to serve his own senseless ambitions... .

Only last night the Polish Ambassador did see the German Foreign Secretary, Herr von Ribbentrop. Once again he expressed to him what, indeed, the Polish Government had already said publicly: that they were willing to negotiate with Germany about their disputes on an equal basis.

What was the reply of the German Government? The reply was that without another word the German troops crossed the Polish frontier this morning at dawn and are since reported to be bombing open towns. In these circumstances there is only one course open to us.

His Majesty's Ambassador in Berlin and the French Ambassador have been instructed to hand to the German Government the following document:

"Early this morning the German Chancellor issued a proclamation to the German army which indicated that he was about to attack Poland. Information which has reached His Majesty's Government in the United Kingdom and the French Government indicates that attacks upon Polish towns are proceeding. In these circumstances it appears to the governments of the United Kingdom and France that by its action the German Government have created conditions, namely, an aggressive act of force against Poland threatening the independence of Poland, which call for the implementation by the governments of the United Kingdom and France of the undertaking to Poland to come to her assistance. I am accordingly to inform your Excellency that unless the German Government is prepared to give His Majesty's Government satisfactory assurances that the German Government has suspended all aggressive action against Poland and is prepared promptly to withdraw its forces from Polish territory, His Majesty's Government in the United Kingdom will without hesitation fulfill its obligations to Poland."

Yesterday, we took further steps towards the completion of our defensive preparation. This morning we ordered complete mobilization of the whole of the Royal Navy, Army and Royal Air Force. We have also taken a number of other measures, both at home and abroad, which the House will not perhaps expect me to specify in detail. Briefly, they represent the final steps in accordance with prearranged plans.

The thoughts of many of us must at this moment inevitably be turning back to 1914 and to a comparison of our position now with that which existed then. How do we stand this time? The answer is that all three Services are ready and that the situation in all directions is far more favourable and reassuring than in 1914, while behind the fighting Services we have built up a vast organization of Civil Defense under our scheme of Air Raid Precautions.

As regards the immediate manpower requirements, the Royal Navy, the Army and the Air Force are in the fortunate position of having almost as many men as they can conveniently handle at this moment. There are, however, certain categories of service in which men are immediately required, both for military and civil defense. These will be announced in detail through the press and the BBC.

It is essential in the face of the tremendous task which confronts us, more especially in view of our past experiences in this matter, to organize our manpower this time upon as methodical, equitable and economical a basis as possible.

We, therefore, propose immediately to introduce legislation directed to that end. A bill will be laid before you which for all practical purposes will amount to an expansion of the Military Training Act. Under its operation all fit men between the ages of 18 and 41 will be rendered liable to military service if and when called upon. It is not intended at the outset that any considerable number of men other than those already liable shall be called up, and steps will be taken to ensure that the manpower essentially required by industry shall not be taken away.

There is one other allusion which I should like to make before I end my speech, and that is to record my satisfaction of His Majesty's Government, that throughout these last days of crisis Signor Mussolini also has been doing his best to reach a solution. It now only remains for us to set our teeth and to enter upon this struggle, which we ourselves earnestly endeavoured to avoid, with determination to see it through to the end.

We shall enter it with a clear conscience, with the support of the Dominions and the British Empire, and the moral approval of the greater part of the world.

We have no quarrel with the German people, except that they allow themselves to be governed by a Nazi Government. As long as that government exists and pursues the methods it has so persistently followed during the last two years, there will be no peace in Europe. We shall merely pass from one crisis to another, and see one country after another attacked by methods which have now become familiar to us in their sickening technique.

We are resolved that these methods must come to an end. If out of the struggle we again reestablish in the world the rules of good faith and the renunciation of force, why, then even the sacrifices that will be entailed upon us will find their fullest justification.

7. WILLIAM JEFFERSON CLINTON (1946–)

Bill Clinton, a Democrat leader, was the forty-second US president. He was elected in 1993 and re-elected in 1996.

In this speech, made on 10 June 1999, he announces the end of the war in Kosovo.

*M*y fellow Americans, tonight, for the first time in 79 days, the skies over Yugoslavia are silent. The Serb army and police are withdrawing from Kosovo. The one million men, women and children driven from their land are preparing to return home. The demands of an outraged and united international community have been met.

I can report to the American people that we have achieved a victory for a safer world, for our democratic values, and for a stronger America. Our pilots have returned to base. The air strikes have been suspended. Aggression against an innocent people has been contained and is being turned back.

When I ordered our armed forces into combat, we had three clear goals: to enable the Kosovar people, the victims of some of the most vicious atrocities in Europe since the Second World War, to return to their homes with safety and self-government; to require Serbian forces responsible for those atrocities to leave Kosovo; and to deploy an international security force, with NATO at its core, to protect all the people of that troubled land, Serbs and Albanians alike. Those goals will be achieved. Unnecessary conflict has been brought to a just and honourable conclusion. The result will be security and dignity for the people of Kosovo, achieved by an alliance that stood together in purpose and resolve, assisted by the diplomatic efforts of Russia.

This victory brings a new hope that when a people are singled out for destruction because of their heritage and religious faith and we can do something about it, the world will not look the other way.

I want to express my profound gratitude to the men and women of our armed forces and those of our allies. Day after day, night after night, they flew, risking their lives to attack their targets and to avoid civilian casualties when they were fired upon from populated areas. I ask every American to join me in saying to them, "Thank you. You've made us very proud."

I'm also grateful to the American people for standing against the awful ethnic cleansing, for sending generous assistance to the refugees and for opening your hearts and your homes to the innocent victims who came here. I want to speak with you for a few moments tonight about why we fought, what we achieved and what we have to do now to advance the peace and, together with the people of the Balkans, forge a future of freedom, progress and harmony.

We should remember that the violence we responded to in Kosovo was the culmination of a 10-year campaign by Slobodan Milosevic, the leader of Serbia, to exploit ethnic and religious difference in order to impose his will on the lines of the former Yugoslavia. That's what he tried to do in Croatia and Bosnia and now in Kosovo. The world saw the terrifying consequences: five hundred villages burned; men of all ages separated from their loved ones to be shot and buried in mass graves; women raped; children made to watch their parents die; a whole people forced to abandon, in hours, communities their families had spent generations building. For these atrocities, Mr. Milosevic and his top aides have been indicted by the International War Crimes Tribunal for war crimes and crimes against humanity.

There will be no more days of foraging for food in the cold mountains and forests. No more nights of hiding in cellars, wondering if the next day will bring death or deliverance. They will know that Mr. Milosevic's army and paramilitary forces will be gone, his 10 years of repression, finished.

NATO has achieved this success as a united alliance, ably led by Secretary General Solana and General Clark. Nineteen democracies came together and stayed together through the stiffest military challenge in NATO's 50-year history.

We also preserved our critically important partnership with Russia. Thanks to President Yeltsin, who opposed our military effort, but supported diplomacy to end the conflict on terms that met our conditions... . Now, I hope Russian troops will join us in the force that will keep the peace in Kosovo, just as they have in Bosnia.

Finally, we have averted the wider war this conflict might well have sparked. The countries of Southeastern Europe backed the NATO campaign, helped the refugees, and showed the world there is more compassion than cruelty in this troubled region. This victory makes it all the more likely that they will choose a future of democracy, fair treatment of minorities, and peace.

Now, we're entering a new phase—building that peace—and there are formidable challenges. First, we must be sure the Serbian authorities meet their commitments. We are prepared to resume our military campaign, should they fail to do so.

Next, we must get the Kosovar refugees home safely. Minefields will have to be cleared. Homes destroyed by Serb forces will have to be rebuilt. Homeless people in need of food and medicine will have to get them. The fate of the missing will have to be determined. The Kosovar Liberation Army will have to demilitarize as it has agreed to do. And we in the peacekeeping force will have to ensure that Kosovo is a safe place to live for all its citizens, ethnic Serbs as well as ethnic Albanians.

So we have made sure that the force going into Kosovo will have NATO command and control and rules of engagement set by NATO. It will have the means and the mandate to protect itself while doing its job. In the meantime, the United Nations will organize a civilian administration while preparing the Kosovars to govern and police themselves. As local institutions take hold, NATO will be able to turn over increasing responsibility to them and draw down its forces.

Our third challenge will be to put in place a plan for lasting peace and stability in Kosovo and through all the Balkans. For that to happen, the European Union and the United States must plan for tomorrow, not just today. We must help to give the democracies of Southeastern Europe a path to a prosperous shared future, a unifying magnet more powerful than the pull of hatred and destruction that has threatened to tear them apart. Our European partners must provide most of the resources for this effort, but it is in America's interest to do our part as well.

A final challenge will be to encourage Serbia to join its neighbours in this historic journey, to a peaceful democratic united Europe.

My fellow Americans, all these challenges are substantial, but they are far preferable to the challenges of war and continued instability in Europe. We have sent a message of determination and hope to all the world. Think of all the millions of innocent people who died in this bloody century because democracies reacted too late to evil and aggression.

Because of our resolve, the twentieth century is ending, not with helpless indignation, but with a hopeful affirmation of human dignity and human rights for the twenty-first century. In a world too divided by fear among people of different racial, ethnic and religious groups, we have given confidence to the friends of freedom and pause to those who would exploit human difference for inhuman purposes.

America still faces great challenges in this world, but we look forward to meeting them. So tonight I ask you to be proud of your country and very proud of the men and women who serve it in uniform. For in Kosovo we did the right thing. We did it the right way. And we will finish the job.

Good night and may God bless our wonderful United States of America.

8. EDOUARD DALADIER (1884–1970)

Edouard Daladier was the premier of France during the Second World War.

He delivered this radio address to the people of France on 29 January 1940 just before Hitler's army attacked France.

*A*t the end of five months of war one thing has become more and more clear. It is that Germany seeks to establish a domination over the world completely different from any known in history.

The domination at which the Nazis aim is not limited to the displacement of the balance of power and the imposition of supremacy of one nation. It seeks the systematic and total destruction of those conquered by Hitler, and it does not have a treaty with the nations which he has subdued. He destroys them. He takes from them their whole political and economic existence and seeks even to deprive them of their history and their culture. He wishes to consider them only as vital space and a vacant territory over which he has every right.

The human beings who constitute these nations are for him only cattle. He orders their massacre or their migration. He compels them to make room for their conquerors. He does not even take the trouble to impose any war tribute on them. He just takes all their wealth, and, to prevent any revolt, he wipes out their leaders and scientifically seeks the physical and moral degradation of those whose independence he has taken away.

Under this domination, in thousands of towns and villages in Europe there are millions of human beings now living in misery which, some months ago, they could never have imagined. Austria, Bohemia, Slovakia and Poland are only lands of despair. Their whole peoples have been deprived of the means of moral and material happiness. Subdued by treachery or brutal violence, they have no other recourse than to work for their executioners who grant them scarcely enough to assure the most miserable existence.

There is being created a world of masters and slaves in the image of Germany herself. For, while Germany is crushing beneath her tyranny the men of every race and language, she is herself being crushed beneath her own servitude and her domination mania. The German workers and peasants are the slaves of their Nazi masters while the workers and peasants of Bohemia and Poland have become in turn slaves of these slaves. Before this first realisation of a mad dream, the whole world might shudder.

Nazi propaganda is entirely founded on the exploitation of the weakness of the human heart. It does not address itself to the strong or the heroic. It tells the rich they are going to lose their money. It tells the worker this is a rich man's war. It tells the intellectual and the artist that all he cherished is being destroyed by war. It tells the lover of good things that soon he would have none of them. It says to the Christian believer: "How can you accept this massacre?" It tells the adventurer: "A man like you should profit by the misfortunes of your country."

It is those who speak this way who have destroyed or confiscated all the wealth they could lay their hands on, who have reduced their workers to slavery, who have ruined all intellectual liberty, who have imposed terrible privations on millions of men and women and who have made murder their law. What do contradictions matter to them if they can lower the resistance of those who wish to bar the path of their ambitions to be masters of the world?

For us there is more to do than merely win the war. We shall win it, but we must also win a victory far greater than that of arms. In this world of masters and slaves, which those madmen who rule at Berlin are seeking to forge, we must also save liberty and human dignity.

9. FREDERICK DOUGLASS (1817–1895)

Frederick Douglass, the best known and the most influential African American leader of the 1800s, was a leading figure in the New England anti-slavery movement.

He gave this scathing speech when invited by the citizens of Rochester to address their Fourth of July celebrations in 1852.

*F*ellow citizens, pardon me, and allow me to ask, why am I called upon to speak here today? What have I, or those I represent, to do with your national independence? Are the great principles of political freedom and of natural justice, embodied in that Declaration of Independence, extended to us? And am I, therefore, called upon to bring our humble offering to the national altar, and to confess the benefits and express devout gratitude for the blessings resulting from your independence to us?

Would to God, both for your sakes and ours, that an affirmative answer could be truthfully returned to these questions. Then would my task be light, and my burden easy and delightful. But such is not the state of the case. I say it with a sad sense of disparity between us. I am not included within the pale of this glorious anniversary! Your high independence only reveals the immeasurable distance between us. The blessings in which you this day rejoice are not enjoyed in common. The rich inheritance of justice, liberty, prosperity and independence, bequeathed by your fathers, is shared by you, not by me. This Fourth of July is yours, not mine. You may rejoice, I must mourn.

Fellow citizens, above your national, tumultuous joy, I hear the mournful wail of millions, whose chains, heavy and grievous yesterday, are today rendered more intolerable by the jubilant shouts that reach them. To forget them, to pass lightly over their wrongs and to chime in with the popular theme would be treason most scandalous and shocking, and would make me a reproach before God and the world.

My subject, then, fellow citizens, is "American Slavery". I shall see this day and its popular characteristics from the slave's point of view. Standing here, identified with the American bondman, making his wrongs mine, I do not hesitate to declare, with all my soul, that the character and conduct of this nation never looked blacker to me than on this Fourth of July.

Whether we turn to the declarations of the past, or to the professions of the present, the conduct of the nation seems equally hideous and revolting. America is false to the past, false to the present, and solemnly binds herself to be false to the future. I will use the severest language I can command, and yet not one word shall escape me that any man, whose judgment is not blinded by prejudice, or who is not at heart a slave-holder, shall not confess to be right and just.

What point in the anti-slavery creed would you have me argue? On what branch of the subject do the people of this country need light? Must I undertake to prove that the slave is a man? That point is conceded already. Nobody doubts it.

What! Am I to argue that it is wrong to make men brutes, to rob them of their liberty, to work them without wages, to keep them ignorant of their relations to their fellow men, to beat them with sticks, to flay their flesh with the lash, to load their limbs with irons, to hunt them with dogs, to sell them at auction, to sunder their families, to knock out their teeth, to burn their flesh, to starve them into obedience and submission to their masters? Must I argue that a system thus marked with blood and stained with pollution is wrong? No—I will not. I have better employment for my time and strength than such arguments would imply.

What, then, remains to be argued? Is it that slavery is not divine; that God did not establish it; that our doctors of divinity are mistaken? There is blasphemy in the thought. That which is inhuman cannot be divine. Who can reason on such a proposition? They that can, may—I cannot. The time for such argument is past.

What to the American slave is your Fourth of July? I answer: a day that reveals to him more than all other days of the year, the gross injustice and cruelty to which he is the constant victim. To him your celebration is a sham; your boasted liberty, an unholy licence; your national greatness, swelling vanity; your sounds of rejoicing are empty and heartless; your shouts of liberty and equality, hollow mock; your prayers and hymns, your sermons and thanksgivings, with all your religious parade and solemnity, are to him mere bombast, fraud, deception, impiety, and hypocrisy—a thin veil to cover up crimes which would disgrace a nation of savages. There is not a nation of the earth guilty of practices more shocking and bloody than are the people of these United States at this very hour.

Go search where you will, roam through all the monarchies and despotisms of the Old World, travel through South America, search out every abuse and when you have found the last, lay your facts by the side of the everyday practices of this nation, and you will say with me that, for revolting barbarity and shameless hypocrisy, America reigns without a rival.

10. DWIGHT D EISENHOWER (1890–1969)

General Dwight Eisenhower was the Republican president of the US from 1953 to 1961. He was commander-in-chief of the Allied forces in the years 1943–1945 in the European theatre of operations. This is his farewell speech given on 17 January 1961.

*M*y fellow Americans:
This evening I come to you with a message of leave-taking and farewell, and to share a few final thoughts with you, my countrymen. Like every other citizen, I wish the new president, and all who will labour with him, Godspeed. I pray that the coming years will be blessed with peace and prosperity for all.

We now stand ten years past the midpoint of a century that has witnessed four major wars among great nations. Three of these involved our own country. Despite these holocausts America is today the strongest, the most influential and the most productive nation in the world. Understandably proud of this preeminence, we yet realise that America's leadership and prestige depend, not merely upon our unmatched material progress, riches and military strength, but on how we use our power in the interests of world peace and human betterment.

Progress toward these noble goals is persistently threatened by the conflict now engulfing the world. It commands our whole attention, absorbs our very beings. We face a hostile ideology global in scope, atheistic in character, ruthless in purpose, and insidious in method. Unhappily, the danger it poses promises to be of indefinite duration. To meet it successfully, there is called for, not so much the emotional and transitory sacrifices of crisis, but rather those which enable us to carry forward steadily, surely, and without complaint the burdens of a prolonged and complex struggle—with liberty the stake. Only thus shall we remain, despite every provocation, on our charted course toward permanent peace and human betterment.

A vital element in keeping the peace is our military establishment. Our arms must be mighty, ready for instant action, so that no potential aggressor may be tempted to risk his own destruction. Our military organisation today bears little relation to that known by any of my predecessors in peacetime, or indeed by the fighting men of World War II or Korea.

Until the latest of our world conflicts, the United States had no armaments industry. American makers of plowshares could, with time and as required, make swords as well. But now we can no longer risk emergency improvisation of national defence; we have been compelled to create a permanent armaments industry of vast proportions. Added to this, three and a half million men and women are directly engaged in the defence establishment. We annually spend on military security more than the net income of all United States corporations.

This conjunction of an immense military establishment and a large arms industry is new in the American experience. The total influence—economic, political, even spiritual—is felt in every city, every State house, every office of the federal government. We recognise the imperative need for this development. Yet we must not fail to comprehend its grave implications. Our toil, resources and livelihood are all involved; so is the very structure of our society.

In the councils of government, we must guard against the acquisition of unwarranted influence, whether sought or unsought, by the military-industrial complex. The potential for the disastrous rise of misplaced power exists and will persist. We must never let the weight of this combination endanger our liberties or democratic processes. We should take nothing for granted. Only an alert and knowledgeable citizenry can compel the proper meshing of the huge industrial and military machinery of defence with our peaceful methods and goals, so that security and liberty may prosper together. Akin to, and largely responsible for the sweeping changes in our industrial-military posture, has been the technological revolution during recent decades.

In this revolution, research has become central, it also becomes more formalised, complex, and costly. A steadily increasing share is conducted for, by, or at the direction of, the federal government.

Today, the solitary inventor, tinkering in his shop, has been overshadowed by task forces of scientists in laboratories and testing fields. In the same fashion, the free university, historically the fountainhead of free ideas and scientific discovery, has experienced a revolution in the conduct of research. Partly because of the huge costs involved, a government contract becomes virtually a substitute for intellectual curiosity. For every old blackboard there are now hundreds of new electronic computers.

The prospect of domination of the nation's scholars by federal employment, project allocations, and the power of money is ever present — and is gravely to be regarded. Yet, in holding scientific research and discovery in respect, as we should, we must also be alert to the equal and opposite danger that public policy could itself become the captive of a scientific-technological elite. It is the task of statesmanship to mold, to balance, and to integrate these and other forces, new and old, within the principles of our democratic system — ever aiming toward the supreme goals of our free society.

Another factor in maintaining balance involves the element of time. As we peer into society's future, we — you and I, and our government — must avoid the impulse to live only for today, plundering for our own ease and convenience, the precious resources of tomorrow. We cannot mortgage the material assets of our grandchildren without asking the loss also of their political and spiritual heritage. We want democracy to survive for all generations to come, not to become the insolvent phantom of tomorrow.

Down the long lane of the history yet to be written, America knows that this world of ours, ever growing smaller, must avoid becoming a community of dreadful fear and hate, and be, instead, a proud confederation of mutual trust and respect.

11. WILLIAM FAULKNER (1897–1962)

American novelist William Faulkner won the Nobel Prize for literature in 1949.
He gave the following speech on receiving the Nobel Prize.

$\mathcal{G}$ feel that this award was not made to me as a man but to my work—a life's work in the agony and sweat of the human spirit, not for glory and least of all for profit, but to create out of materials of the human spirit something which did not exists before. So this award is only mine in trust.

It will not be difficult to find a declaration for the money part of it commensurate with the purpose and significance of its origin. But I would like to do the same with the acclaim, too, by using this moment as a pinnacle from which might be listened to by the young men and women already dedicated to the same anguish and travail, among whom is already that one who will some day stand where I am standing.

Our tragedy today is a general and universal physical fear so long sustained by now that we can even bear it. There are no longer problems of the spirit. There is only the question: When will I be blown up? Because of this the young man or woman writing today has forgotten the problems of the human heart in conflict with itself which alone could make good writing because only that is worth writing about, worth the agony and the sweat.

He must learn them again. He must teach himself that the basest of all things is to be afraid and teaching himself that, forget it forever, leaving no room in his workshop for anything but the old verities and truths of the heart—the universal truths lacking which any story is ephemeral and doomed—love and honour and pity and pride and compassion and sacrifice.

Until he does, he labours under a course. He writes not of love but of lust, of defeats in which nobody loses anything of value, of victories without hope and worst of all without pity or compassion. His griefs grieve on no universal bones, leaving no scars. He writes not of the heart but of the glands.

Until he learns these things, he will write as though he stood among and watched the end of man. I decline to accept the end of man. It is easy enough to say that man is immortal simply because he will endure, that when the last ding dong of doom has clanged and faded from the last worthless rock hanging tideless in the last red and dying evening, that even then there will still be one more sound: that of his puny inexhaustible voice, still talking. I refuse to accept this.

I believe that man will not merely endure; he will prevail. His is immortal not because he alone among creatures has an inexhaustible voice, but because he has a soul, a spirit capable of compassion and sacrifice and endurance.

The poet's, writer's duty is to write about these things. It is his privilege to help man endure by lifting his heart, by reminding him of the courage and honour and hope and pride and compassion and pity and sacrifice which have been the glory of his past. The poet's voice need not merely by the record of man, it can be one props, the pillars to help him endure and prevail.

12. GERALD R FORD (1913–)

Gerald Ford was the American Republican president from 1974 to 1977.

This speech was given by him amid the international turmoil surrounding the end of the Vietnam War, on 23 April 1975, while 100,000 North Vietnamese soldiers were advancing toward Saigon, South Vietnam's capital.

It is really a great privilege and a very high honour to have an opportunity of participating again in a student activity at Tulane University. And for this opportunity, I thank you very, very much.

When I had the privilege of speaking here in 1968 at your "Directions '68" forum, I had no idea that my own career and our entire nation would move so soon in another direction. And I say again, I am extremely proud to be invited back.

I am impressed, as I undoubtedly said before – but I would reiterate it tonight – by Tulane's unique distinction as the only American university to be converted from state sponsorship to private status. And I am also impressed by the Tulane graduates who serve in the United States Congress: Bennett Johnston, Lindy Boggs, Dave Treen. I think the fact that you have these three outstanding graduates testifies to the academic excellence and the inspiration of this historic university, rooted in the past with its eyes on the future.

Just as Tulane has made a great transition from the past to the future, so has New Orleans, the legendary city that has made such a unique contribution to our great America. New Orleans is more, as I see it, than weathered bricks and cast-iron balconies. It is an example of retention of a very special culture in a progressive environment of modern change.

On January 8, 1815, a monumental American victory was achieved here—the Battle of New Orleans. Louisiana had been a state for less than three years, but outnumbered Americans innovated, outnumbered Americans used the tactics of the frontier to defeat a veteran British force trained in the strategy of the Napoleonic wars.

We as a nation had suffered humiliation and a measure of defeat in the War of 1812. Our National Capital in Washington had been captured and burned. So, the illustrious victory in the Battle of New Orleans was a powerful restorative to our national pride.

Today, America can regain the sense of pride that existed before Vietnam. But it cannot be achieved by refighting a war that is finished as far as America is concerned. As I see it, the time has come to look forward to an agenda for the future, to unify, to bind up the nation's wounds, and to restore its health and its optimistic self-confidence.

I ask that we stop refighting the battles and the recriminations of the past. I ask that we look now at what is right with America, at our possibilities and our potentialities for change and growth and achievement and sharing. I ask that we accept the responsibilities of leadership as a good neighbour to all peoples and the enemy of none. I ask that we strive to become, in the finest American tradition, something more tomorrow than we are today.

We, of course, are saddened indeed by the events in Indo-China. But these events, tragic as they are, portend neither the end of the world nor of America's leadership in the world.

Let me put it this way, if I might. Some tend to feel that if we do not succeed in everything everywhere, then we have succeeded in nothing anywhere. I reject categorically such polarised thinking. We can and we should help others to help themselves. But the fate of responsible men and women everywhere, in the final decision, rests in their own hands, not in ours.

America's future depends upon Americans—especially your generation, which is now equipping itself to assume the challenges of the future, to help write the agenda for America.

Abraham Lincoln asked, in his own words, and I quote, "What constitutes the bulwark of our own liberty and independence?" And he answered, "It is not our frowning battlements or bristling seacoasts, our army or our navy. Our defence is in the spirit which prized liberty as the heritage of all men, in all lands everywhere." It is in this spirit that we must now move beyond the discords of the past decade. It is in this spirit that I ask you to join me in writing an agenda for the future.

I welcome your invitation particularly tonight, because I know it is at Tulane and other centers of thought throughout our great country that much consideration is being given to the kind of future Americans want and, just as importantly, will work for. Each of you are preparing yourselves for the future, and I am deeply interested in your preparations and your opinions and your goals. However, tonight, with your indulgence, let me share with you my own views.

I envision a creative programme that goes as far as our courage and our capacities can take us, both at home and abroad. My goal is for a cooperative world at peace, using its resources to build, not to destroy.

As president, I am determined to offer leadership to overcome our current economic problems. My goal is jobs for all who want to work and economic opportunity for all who want to achieve. I am determined to seek self-sufficiency in energy as an urgent national priority. My goal is to make America independent of foreign energy sources by 1985. Of course, I will pursue interdependence with other nations and a reformed international economic system. My goal is for a world in which consuming and producing nations achieve a working balance.

I will address the humanitarian issues of hunger and famine, of health and of healing. My goal is to achieve — or to assure — basic needs and an effective system to achieve this result. I recognise the need for technology that enriches life while preserving our natural environment. My goal is to stimulate productivity, but use technology to redeem, not to destroy our environment.

I will strive for new cooperation rather than conflict in the peaceful exploration of our oceans and our space. My goal is to use resources for peaceful progress rather than war and destruction. Let America symbolise humanity's struggle to conquer nature and master technology. The time has now come for our government to facilitate the individual's control over his or her future — and of the future of America.

But the future requires more than Americans congratulating themselves on how much we know and how many products that we can produce. It requires new knowledge to meet new problems. We must not only be motivated to build a better America, we must know how to do it.

If we really want a humane America that will, for instance, contribute to the alleviation of the world's hunger, we must realise that good intentions do not feed people. Yet, the world economy has become interdependent. Not only food technology but money management, natural resources and energy, research and development—all kinds of this group require an organised world society that makes the maximum effective use of the world's resources.

I want to tell the world: Let's grow food together, but let's also learn more about nutrition, about weather forecasting, about irrigation, about the many other specialties involved in helping people to help themselves.

As we strive together to perfect a new agenda, I put high on the list of important points the maintenance of alliances and partnerships with other people and other nations. These do provide a basis of shared values, even as we stand up with determination for what we believe. This, of course, requires a continuing commitment to peace and a determination to use our good offices wherever possible to promote better relations between nations of this world.

The new agenda, that which is developed by you and by us, must place a high priority on the need to stop the spread of nuclear weapons and to work for the mutual reduction in strategic arms and control of other weapons.

I am glad that Tulane University and other great American educational institutions are reaching out to others in programmes to work with developing nations, and I look forward with confidence to your participation in every aspect of America's future.

And I urge Americans of all ages to unite in this Bicentennial year, to take responsibility for themselves as our ancestors did. Let us resolve tonight to rediscover the old virtues of confidence and self-reliance and capability that characterised our forefathers two centuries ago. I pledge, as I know you do, each one of us, to do our part.

Let the beacon light of the past shine forth from historic New Orleans and from Tulane University and from every other corner of this land to illuminate a boundless future for all Americans and a peace for all mankind.

Thank you very much.

13. INDIRA GANDHI (1917–1984)

Indira Gandhi holds the distinction of being the world's first woman to head an elected government. She was India's prime minister from 1966 to 1977, and from 1980 to 1984.

This is her address to the Plenary Meeting of Non-Aligned Countries at the United Nations, New York, on 26 September 1983.

The world situation is far more complex than our collective appraisal of it.... Tensions, mistrust and confrontation between the great powers are rising. Even the words in which they address each other are increasingly inflexible, threatening and condemnatory. The very fabric of international peace is under serious stress. The world stands a helpless witness to a major escalation of the nuclear arms race.

Against this sombre background, I believe this coming together of statesmen from different parts of the world in a search for peace, disarmament and development is indeed timely and essential.

Obviously, disarmament must remain high on the list of priorities of all nations and even individuals who are anxious about the human race and our beautiful planet, who consider peace, security and stability indispensable to human survival and progress to higher levels.

Our goal is general and complete disarmament, a process which must necessarily bring peace with nuclear disarmament. At the moment the trend is in the opposite direction — of expanding existing arsenals. Disarmament cannot make any progress until this process is reversed. The first need is to stop the production of nuclear weapons, then reduce and eventually eliminate them. The Non-Aligned Movement has also made some other important proposals involving, *inter alia*, an international convention prohibiting the use or threat of use of nuclear weapons, which has been endorsed by the General Assembly. However discouraging the response of those directly concerned, we cannot afford to slacken our efforts.

Several political issues also demand our urgent attention. Peace in West Asia remains of paramount concern. It must be based on a just and durable settlement of the questions at the core of the problems, Israeli aggression and the self-determination or a nationhood for the Palestinian people. The valiant and oppressed people of Namibia also look to us for continued solidarity and support. The independence of Namibia cannot be thwarted or delayed through the projection of great power interests, or by linking it with extraneous considerations. The United Nations has special responsibility in this regard. We should like to see it exert its great authority fully in resolving these issues.

We are worried about Lebanon. It is good that a cease-fire has been announced. Lebanon has not had peace and tranquillity for many years. Its current troubles are largely due to last year's Israeli aggression. Israel must withdraw completely from Lebanon. We, the non-aligned, support the unity and territorial integrity of Lebanon and the withdrawal of all foreign forces.

Events in Central America, the acts of provocation and aggression which tend to aggravate tensions cannot but cause grave concern to non-aligned countries. I hope, the United Nations will continue to support the Contadora initiative for a peaceful resolution of the problems of this troubled region.

Another important question that has engaged our attention is the unfortunate and unresolved conflict between Iran and Iraq which has sapped the strength of both countries and taken a heavy toll of human lives on both sides.

At the centre of the current crisis lies the inability of the outdated and inequitable international monetary and financial system to deal with the current and future needs of the economy of the world and particularly of the developing countries. The only effective way out is a comprehensive reform of the existing system through an international conference on money and finance.

A just and equitable international economic order is the very foundation of world peace and tranquillity in international relations.

In terms of membership and global spread, the Non-Aligned Movement represents today the world's biggest strand in international politics. Comprising about two-third member-states of the United Nations system, the Non-Aligned states have been playing an increasingly dominant and often a decisive role not only in the General Assembly of the United Nations, but also in regional and global peace.

The United Nations and NAM have reinforced each other in many ways. Their membership has increased in an interacting manner—increase in one resulting in increase in the other. The major concerns of the United Nations and the NAM have been shared since the seventies in a more pronounced manner, the diction, rhetoric and emphasis of the majority of members have been quite similar. In fact, the United Nations has become a principal forum of the NAM, where its members outnumber and can, and occasionally did, outvote other groupings. No other grouping of states has had such an obvious and a decisive impact an the working of the United Nations as the group of countries comprising the NAM. Both as a group and as individual members, over the years, even when they were in a minority, and some—India, Yugoslavia and Egypt—even prior to the formal establishment of NAM in 1961, influenced the working of the United Nations in many ways: in the preparation of the agenda, the direction of committee work, the form and substance of resolution, the style and manner of UN action and the general trend of collective activities of the UN and its many agencies. It is with the sense of pride and identity that NAM has with the UN, and President Tito, in what was probably his last appearance, recognised it as a real support to "the realisation of the university of the UN and to the strengthening of its role and importance."

The NAM has thus a structure that provides a forum for articulating its demands in the global community and offers its members an institutional format for negotiations on certain issues of concern. It is because of the United Nations system that NAM has acquired its international legitimacy and universal recognition as a group, large though disparate, that represents the bulk of humanity as congregated in the three continents of Asia, Africa and Latin America, and cluster of islands in the seas and oceans of the world.

14. MOHANDAS KARAMCHAND GANDHI
(1869–1948)

Mahatma Gandhi, also known as Father of the Nation, led India to independence. He was voted as one of the greatest personalities of the twentieth century.

The following is the famous Quit India speech that he delivered on 8 August 1942.

*B*efore you discuss the resolution, let me place before you one or two things. I want you to understand two things very clearly and to consider them from the same point of view from which I am placing them before you. I ask you to consider it from my point of view, because if you approve of it, you will be enjoined to carry out all I say. It will be a great responsibility. There are people who ask me whether I am the same man that I was in 1920, or whether there has been any change in me. You are right in asking that question.

Let me, however, hasten to assure that I am the same Gandhi as I was in 1920. I have not changed in any fundamental respect. I attach the same importance to nonviolence that I did then. If at all, my emphasis on it has grown stronger. There is no real contradiction between the present resolution and my previous writings and utterances.

Occasions like the present do not occur in everybody's and, but rarely, in anybody's life. I want you to know and feel that there is nothing but purest Ahimsa in all that I am saying and doing today. The draft resolution of the working committee is based on Ahimsa. The contemplated struggle, similarly, has its roots in Ahimsa. If, therefore, there is any among you who has lost faith in Ahimsa or is wearied of it, let him not vote for this resolution.

Let me explain my position clearly. God has vouchsafed to me a priceless gift in the weapon of Ahimsa. I and my Ahimsa are on our trail today. If in the present crisis, when the earth is being scorched by the flames of Himsa and crying for deliverance, I failed to make use of the God-given talent, God will not forgive me and I shall be judged un-wrongly of the great gift. I must act now. I may not hesitate and merely look on when Russia and China are threatened.

Ours is not a drive for power, but purely a nonviolent fight for India's independence. In a violent struggle, a successful general has been often known to effect a military coup and to setup a dictatorship. But under the Congress scheme of things, essentially nonviolent as it is, there can be no room for dictatorship. A nonviolent soldier of freedom will covet nothing for himself; he fights only for the freedom of his country. The Congress is unconcerned as to who will rule when freedom is attained. The power, when it comes, will belong to the people of India, and it will be for them to decide to whom it placed in the entrusted. May be that the reins will be placed in the hands of the Parsis, for instance—as I would love to see happen—or they may be handed to some others whose names are not heard in the Congress today. It will not be for you then to object saying, "This community is microscopic. That party did not play its due part in the freedom's struggle; why should it have all the power?" Ever since its inception, the Congress has kept itself meticulously free of the communal taint. It has thought always in terms of the whole nation and has acted accordingly... .

I know how imperfect our Ahimsa is and how far away we are still from the ideal, but in Ahimsa there is no final failure or defeat. I have faith, therefore, that if, in spite of our shortcomings, the big thing does happen, it will be because God wanted to help us by crowning with success our silent, unremitting Sadhana for the last twenty-two years.

I believe that in the history of the world, there has not been a more genuinely democratic struggle for freedom than ours. I read Carlyle's French Resolution while I was in prison, and Pandit Jawaharlal has told me something about the Russian revolution. But it is my conviction that inasmuch as these struggles were fought with the weapon of violence, they failed to realise the democratic ideal. In the democracy which I have envisaged—a democracy established by non-violence—there will be equal freedom for all. Everybody will be his own master. It is to join a struggle for such democracy that I invite you today. Once you realize this, you will forget the differences between the Hindus and Muslims, and think of yourselves as Indians only, engaged in the common struggle for independence.

Then, there is the question of your attitude towards the British. I have noticed that there is hatred towards the British among the people. The people say they are disgusted with their behaviour. The people make no distinction between British imperialism and the British people. To them, the two are one. This hatred would even make them welcome the Japanese. It is most dangerous. It means that they will exchange one slavery for another. We must get rid of this feeling. Our quarrel is not with the British people. We fight their imperialism. The proposal for the withdrawal of British power did not come out of anger. It came to enable India to play its due part at the present critical juncture. It is not a happy position for a big country like India to be merely helping with money and material obtained willy-nilly from her while the United Nations are conducting the war. We cannot evoke the true spirit of sacrifice and valour, so long as we are not free. I know the British Government will not be able to withhold freedom from us when we have made enough self-sacrifice. We must, therefore, purge ourselves of hatred. Speaking for myself, I can say that I have never felt any hatred. As a matter of fact, I feel myself to be a greater friend of the British now than ever before. One reason is that they are today in distress. My very friendship, therefore, demands that I should try to save them from their mistakes. As I view the situation—they are on the brink of an abyss. It, therefore, becomes my duty to warn them of their danger even though it may, for the time being, anger them to the point of cutting off the friendly hand that is stretched out to help them. People may laugh. Nevertheless, that is my claim. At a time when I may have to launch the biggest struggle of my life, I may not harbour hatred against anybody.

15. GIUSEPPE GARIBALDI (1807–1882)

Garibaldi was an Italian general and a patriot, who, with Mazzini and Cavour, created a united Italy.
He addressed the following speech to his soldiers in 1860 to conquer Italy.

We must now consider the period which is just drawing to a close as almost the last stage of our national resurrection, and prepare ourselves to finish worthily the marvellous design of the elect of twenty generations, the completion of which Providence has reserved for this fortunate age.

Yes, young men, Italy owes to you an undertaking which has merited the applause of the universe. You have conquered and you will conquer still, because you are prepared for the tactics that decide the fate of battles. You are not unworthy of the men who entered the ranks of a Macedonian phalanx, and who contended, not in vain, with the proud conquerors of Asia. To this wonderful page in our country's history, another more glorious still will be added, and the slave shall show at last to his free brothers a sharpened sword forged from the links of his fetters.

To arms, then, all of you! All of you! And the oppressors and the mighty shall disappear like dust. You, too, women, cast away all the cowards from your embraces; they will give you only cowards for children, and you who are the daughters of the land of beauty must bear children who are noble and brave. Let timid doctrinaires depart from among us to carry their servility and their miserable fears elsewhere. This people is its own master. It wishes to be the brother of other peoples, but to look on the insolent with a proud glance, not to grovel before them imploring its own freedom. It will no longer follow in the trail of men whose hearts are foul. No! No! No!

Providence has presented Italy with Victor Emmanuel. Every Italian should rally round him. By the side of Victor Emmanuel every quarrel should be forgotten, all rancour depart. Once more I repeat my battle-cry: To arms, all—all of you! If March 1861 does not find one million of Italians in arms, then, alas for liberty! Alas for the life of Italy! Ah, no. Far be from me a thought which I loathe like poison. March of 1861, or if need be February, will find us all at our post—Italians of Calatafimi, Palermo, Ancona, the Volturno, Castelfidardo, and Isernia, and with us every man of this land who is not a coward or a slave. Let all of us rally round the glorious hero of Paestro and give the last blow to the crumbling edifice of tyranny. Receive, then, my gallant young volunteers, at the honoured conclusion of ten battles, one word of farewell from me.

I utter this word with deepest affection and from the very bottom of my heart. Today I am obliged to retire, but for a few days only. The hour of battle will find me with you again, by the side of the champions of Italian liberty. Let those only return to their homes who are called by the imperative duties which they owe to their families, and those who by their glorious wounds have deserved the credit of their country. These, indeed, will serve Italy in their homes by their counsel, by the very aspect of the scars which adorn their youthful brows. Apart from these, let all others remain to guard our glorious banners. We shall meet again before long to march together to the redemption of our brothers who are still slaves of the stranger. We shall meet again before long to march to new triumphs.

16. BILL GATES (1956–)

Bill Gates is the president and CEO of Microsoft Corporation, and is the world's richest person.

He delivered this speech at Cupertino in California on 17 January 2003, at the Indian Institute of Technology's fiftieth anniversary celebrations.

*W*ell, good evening. It's a great honour for me to speak at this jubilee celebration. After all, I'm not 50-years old, yet, pretty close. I never graduated from college, yet, although I'm not sure I'll be changing that, because I'm a little busy right now, but, I get a chance to talk with you about an incredible institution that has really changed the world and has the potential to do even more in the years ahead than it's already done.

Well, it is quite phenomenal to look back at the start of IIT and realize that a young nation was willing to pour very precious resources into creating this institution. Most people back then didn't understand how important science and engineering would be and yet the early leaders who got behind IIT obviously saw through and knew that the long-term investment would have a huge payout.

Prime Minister Nehru described IIT as representing India's urges, India's future-in-the-making; and, the people here and the other graduates of IIT have made that come true. The impact, of course, has been worldwide, not just on India and the seven campuses but the research and the incredible talent is having a huge impact.

Just one example of that is the incredible revolution taking place in India where literally hundreds of thousands – and in the future, millions – of jobs will be created by taking the educational focus of the country and applying that computer science and high value service type activities and connecting up with the needs for those capabilities not only in India but around the world. It's amazing to see that happening and I think IIT has had a huge role in providing the education and the vision that's led to that wonderful result.

IIT and Microsoft do have a lot in common—an optimism about the future, a belief that fundamental science will lead to breakthroughs that will let us solve some of the toughest problems that mankind faces, a belief that we can provide better tools than ever before and that we've really just scratched the surface.

IIT has certainly taken on a grand vision. Even as an incredibly world-class institution, it keeps challenging itself to renew itself to move to the forefront. And it's hard to think of anything like IIT anywhere in the world. It is a very unique institution.

Microsoft has given over US$7.5 million of its grants to IIT, more than to any organisation except some in the US or in the UK because of what we see going on there. We've hired literally hundreds and hundreds of graduates just in the last two years. Over 50 people have come to Microsoft and we're doing our best to increase the number.

We've also decided one way to increase that number is to have a development center in India, and so we've kicked that off and we're expanding that quite rapidly and that's also become a great thing for our employees who come from India. Many of them have chosen now to go back to India and they can keep their career at Microsoft. In fact, that was a key element in our decision to locate a development center there is that it was a way of retaining incredible talent that wanted to be in India.

Despite the distance, we do a lot to host people, have people on sabbaticals at Microsoft, have competitions and encourage our employees also through our matching programme to support IIT and all of its different activities.

The vision that we have we've described as the digital decade—what do we mean by that? Well, we mean that in the year 2000 the number of people who really used digital approaches for lots of everyday things was quite small. For word processing or e-mail you could say there was some penetration there but for most tasks—buying things, taking notes, organising schedules, dealing with music, dealing with photos, really going through budgeting processes—most things were not done on a digital basis.

So the digital decade is something that we're very excited about. It's very transforming. And it requires a bit of patience. It requires laying the infrastructure for these new approaches. It requires simplifying things. Just because these great things work doesn't mean that they'll be used very broadly.

There is a basic approach in terms of how all these devices find each other and talk to each other, called Web services, that we're also very optimistic about. It's very state-of-the-art distributing computing work. It's a standardized set of protocols that companies like IBM and Microsoft are working on together. We've committed all our R&D to this approach because we see it as not only the foundation for e-commerce but also solving all the tough manageability problems and data exchange problems that we've had in these systems.

One of the biggest challenges we all face to make the digital decade a reality are the issues around trustworthy computing. After all, the kind of reliability we get out of the water system or electricity system, at least in this country, are good enough that we just take them for granted, and we have to have that same capability into this digital infrastructure.

And there are many tough problems here. Even the very basic things are not there today. People use passwords. Well, passwords are very easy to guess. People use the same password on consumer websites they use in their office and it's simply not an adequate way to authenticate people. We'll need to move up to smart cards or biometrics.

Mail protocols: you don't actually know when you get a piece of electronic mail that it really came from the person it purports to. Now, it's a very solvable problem. Again, deep research coming out of academia will be part of it. It won't be solved overnight. Just like a lot of these tough problems, it will take most of this decade to do it, but it's something that absolutely has to be done.

There's certainly an opportunity for IIT, and I expect IIT will seize that to be at the forefront of that and define exactly how that can be used to get great education out to more people and improve the experience, including the experience after you graduate, when you want to renew your skills and be kept up to date on the latest things going on. It's possible that over time graduates of IIT will be constantly in touch with IIT, not just as a group of alumni but also in terms of their ongoing education.

Just last year, late in the year, I had an opportunity to make a trip to India — and it was a wonderful trip. I had a chance to see partners like Infosys. And I got a chance to see our development center and look at how rapidly the computer software and engineering and services businesses are developing in India and share my views and understand how Microsoft can help with that more.

So where do we go from here? Well, I think it's quite clear that the theme I will strike tonight is working together: the United States working with India, commercial organisations like Microsoft working with IIT; and all of us taking these great advances in science and thinking what we can each do to make sure that not only are these great advances available to the developed countries and the luckiest of us all but to the entirety of humanity.

So with that, let me say I'm very optimistic that we will work together and being here with this incredibly talented group, talking about this incredible institution, just makes me all the more optimistic about that. Thank you.

17. CHARLES DE GAULLE (1890–1970)

General de Gaulle was a French general and statesman. He was the
first president of the Fifth Republic, from 1959 to 1969.
   The following is a broadcast made on 18 June 1940 from London,
where he sought asylum.

The leaders, who for the many years past, have been at the
head of the French armed forces have set up a government.
   Alleging the defect of our armies, this government has entered
into negotiations with the enemy with a view to bringing about
a cessation of the hostilities. It is quite true that we were, and still
are, overwhelmed by enemy mechanised forces, both on the
ground and in the air.
   It was the tanks, the planes, and the tactics of the Germans,
for more than the fact that we were outnumbered, that forced
our armies to retreat. It was the German tanks, planes and tactics
that provided the element of surprise which brought our leaders
to their present plight.
   But has the lost word been said? Must we abandon all hope?
Is our defeat final and irremediable? To those questions I answer —
No!
   Speaking in full knowledge of the facts, I ask you to believe
me when I say that the cause of France is not lost. The very
factors that brought about our defeat may one day lead us to
victory.
   For remember this, France does not stand alone. She is not
isolated. Behind her is a vast empire, and she can make common
cause with the British empire, which commands the seas and is
continuing the struggle. Like England, she can draw unreservedly
on the immense industrial resource of the United States.
   This war is not limited to our unfortunate country. The
outcome of the struggle has not been decided by the Battle of

France. This is world war. Mistakes have been made. There have been delays and untold sufferings. But the fact remains that there still exists in the world everything we need to crush our enemies someday.

Today we are crushed by the sheer weight of mechanised force hurled against us, but we can still look to a future in which even mechanised force will bring us victory. The destiny of the world is at stake.

I, General de Gaulle, now in London, call on all French officers and men who are at present on British soil, or may be in the future, with or without their arms. I call on all engineers and skilled workmen from the armament factories who are at present on British soil, or may be in the future, to get in touch with me.

Whatever happens, the flame of French resistance must not, and, shall not, die.

18. MIKHAIL GORBACHEV (1931–)

Mickhail Gorbachev was a Soviet leader who was largely responsible for the political transformation in Eastern Europe in 1989.

The following speech delivered at Leeds on September 1988 focuses on Perestroika and the new role for the third world in the international community.

The emergence into the international arena of over a hundred Asian, African and Latin American countries, which have embarked upon the path of independent development, is one of the great realities of the present-day world. We acclaim this twentieth-century phenomenon. This is a huge and diverse world with vast interests and difficult problems. We realise that the future of civilisation hinges on how this world develops.

The responsibility for these dozens of countries with their aggregate population of many millions, and the responsibility for harnessing their enormous potential for the benefit of world progress, does not lie with them alone.

On the one hand, in the Third World we see examples of rapid, albeit uneven and painful, economic growth. Many countries are becoming modern industrialised states, and several are growing into great powers. The independent policy of most Third World states, which rests upon acquired national dignity, is increasingly affecting international affairs as a whole.

On the other hand, poverty, inhuman living conditions, illiteracy and ignorance, malnutrition and hunger, alarming child mortality, and epidemics remain common features of life for the two and a half billion people who inhabit these former colonies and semi-colonies. Such is the bitter truth. In the early eighties, the per capita income in Third World countries was eleven times lower than that in the industrialised capitalist countries. This gap is widening rather than narrowing.

Nevertheless, the rich Western states continue to collect neocolonialist "tribute". Over the past decade alone, the profits US corporations have siphoned off from the developing countries have quadrupled investments. Americans may call this profitable business. We appraise the situation differently. But I'll go into that later.

The developing countries bear the burden of an enormous external debt. When combined with the volume of the profits taken out every year, the growing debt spells a bleak development outlook and the inevitable aggravation of social, economic and other problems that are already extremely serious.

I recall a conversation I had with President Mitterrand. It boiled down to the following. Clearly, each capitalist enterprise strives for maximum profit. However, a capitalist or a company is forced, largely under worker pressure, to reckon with the fact that, if the enterprise is to function effectively, it is imperative that employees' incomes are guaranteed, and, despite their production capacities, maintain their health, upgrade their qualifications, and raise their children. The capitalist is forced to do this, realising that in doing so he is ensuring himself profit today and tomorrow. But capitalism taken as a whole, represented by the Western countries, does not want to understand even this simple truth in its relations with its former colonies. Capitalism has brought economic relations with Asia, Africa and Latin America to a point where entire nations are doomed to economic stagnation, unable to meet their own essential needs, and bogged down in monstrous debts.

These countries will be unable, of course, to pay back the debts under the present conditions. If a fair solution is not found, anything could happen. The debt of the developing counties has turned into a time bomb of sorts. Detonation could have desperate results. A social explosion of tremendous destructive force is accumulating.

The developing countries' debt is one of the most serious problems in the world. It has been in existence for a long time. But it was either put off, overlooked or discussed in general terms. Western leaders underestimate the danger; they refuse to see the seriousness of the economic upheavals that may happen. This is why they propose half-baked measures and attempt to salvage the situation with palliatives. There is a patent reluctance to take real, substantial steps to normalise economic cooperation with the developing countries.

Extensive efforts are required if genuine changes are to be made and a new world economic order established. It will be a long and hard road, and one has to be prepared for any unexpected turn. The restructuring of international relations demands that the interests of all countries be considered. It requires a balancing of interests, but many do not want to give away anything of their own.

The dire state of the developing countries is the real reason for many of the conflicts in Asia, Africa and Latin America. Discussing this with President Reagan at our meeting in Geneva, I told him that first of all one had to realise where regional conflicts come from.

The truth is that, although they are dissimilar in essence and in the nature of the opposing forces, they usually arise on local soil, as a consequence of internal or regional conflicts which are spawned by the colonial past, new social process, or recurrences of predatory policy, or by all three.

Crises and conflicts are a seedbed for international terrorism. The Soviet Union rejects terrorism in principle and is prepared to cooperate energetically with other states in eradicating this evil. It is expedient to concentrate this work within the United Nations. It would be useful to establish under its aegis a tribunal for investigating acts of international terrorism. During a bilateral dialogue with the Western countries — in the past year there was a major exchange of views on this score between us and the USA, Britain, France, Federal Germany, Italy, Canada and Sweden — we came out for the elaboration of effective measures to combat terrorism. We are prepared to conclude special bilateral agreements. I hope that the front of the common struggle against international terrorism will broaden in the years to come. But one thing is indisputable: if terrorism is to be uprooted, it is imperative to eliminate the reasons that engender conflicts and terrorism.

I have often encountered leading Western politicians who regard the very existence of regional conflicts as the product of "Kremlin conspiratorial activity". How do things really stand?

In the Middle East, a conflict has been in existence between Israel and its neighbours for many years. Moscow is made out to be the culprit, as it invariably stands opposed to Israeli expansion and comes out in defence of the sovereign rights of the Arab peoples, including the Arab people of Palestine. Non-existent anti-Israeli prejudices are ascribed to the Soviet Union, although our country was among the first to promote the formation of the state of Israel.

Important things have to be discussed seriously. The Middle East is a complicated knot in which the interests of many countries are intertwined. The situation there remains dangerous. We believe it to be important for the East and the West that we untie this knot; it is important for the entire world. But there is also the view that the Middle East issues are altogether impossible to resolve. It is difficult even to understand such a position, and it is impossible to agree with it for both political and moral considerations. Logically, the only conclusion that can be drawn is that the situation is bound to be further aggravated, and that there are bound to be new outbreaks of hostilities and more suffering for the people of the region. Wouldn't it be preferable to take an active stand and support the efforts of those who are looking for ways?

Leeds is the fastest growing job magnet in Britain for the 1990s. Competitiveness is about making Britain prosperous and powerful.

I still remember, at that crucial 1981 Test at Headingley, the great Australian bowler Dennis Lillee saying, "I'm betting on England to win." Well, looking around Leeds today and all of you tonight, that is what I am doing: I'm betting on Britain.

19. ADOLF HITLER (1889–1945)

Adolf Hitler was an Austrian-born German dictator, under whose leadership the Nazi party climbed to power. He became the Reich Chancellor in 1933 and the Fuhrer in 1934.
The following speech was addressed to the Germans in 1935.

German fellow citizens:
He who wants to have the deepest impression of the decay and resurrection of Germany most vividly must go and see the development of a city like Wilhelmshaven, which today reverberates with life and activity and which till a short time ago was a dead spot—nearly without means of existence and without prospects of a future. It pays to revisualise this past.

When this city experienced its first upward move, it coincided with the rise. of the German Reich after its unification. Thus, Germany was in a state of peace.

During the time the so-called peace-loving and puritan nations led a great number of wars, Germany had only one aim: to maintain peace, to work in peace, to increase the prosperity of its inhabitants and thereby to contribute to human culture and civilisation.

Even though Germany through the decades was the safest guarantor of peace, and even though she occupied herself with peaceful means, she was unable to prevent other nations from following this rise with envy and hatred and finally had to answer with a war.

We know from numerous findings and publications that in England the conception is that it would be necessary to bring down German military because its destruction would insure every British citizen a greater abundance of life's possessions.

Certainly at that time Germany made mistakes. Its most serious mistake was to see this encirclement and not to slave it off in time.

The only fault we can blame the regime of that time for is that the Reich had full knowledge of this devilish plan of a raid and yet it did not have the power of decision to ward it off in time and could only let this encirclement ripen until the beginning of the catastrophe.

The result was the World War. In this war the German people, although they had by no means the best armaments, fought heroically. No people can claim the glory for itself to have forced us down – much less that nation whose statesmen today speak the greatest words.

Germany at that time remained undefeated and unconquered on land, at sea and in the air. However, it was a weak Germany.

But there was the power of the lie of some nations and the poison of propaganda, which did not balk at misinterpretation and untruth. Thus, Germany faced the world in absolute defencelessness because it was unprepared.

When Wilson's Fourteen Points were published, not only many German fellow-citizens, but above all the "leading" men, saw in these Fourteen Points not only the possibilities of ending the World War, but also the pacification of the world at large. A peace or reconciliation and understanding was promised – a peace that was to know neither victor nor vanquished, a peace of equal justice for all, a peace of equal distribution of colonial domains and equal recognition of colonial desires, a peace that was to be finally crowned by a league of all free nations. It was to be a guarantor of equal rights that would make it seem superfluous in the future for peoples to bear the armaments that previously, so it was said, were so heavily burdensome.

Therefore, disarmament – disarmament of all the nations.

Germany was to go ahead as a good example. Everybody was obliged to follow this disarmament. Also the age of secret diplomacy was to be ended. All problems henceforth were to be discussed openly and freely.

First of all, however, the right of self-determination of nations was to be completely settled and given high priority.

Germany believed in these assurances. With faith in these declarations, it had dropped its weapons. And then a breach of a pledge began, such as world history had never seen before. When our nation had dropped its weapons, a period of supercession, blackmailing, plundering and slavery began. Not another word about peace without victor or vanquished, but an endless sentence of condemnation for the vanquished. Not another word about justice on your side and injustice and illegality on the other. Robbery upon robbery, oppression upon oppression were the consequences. No one in this democratic world bothered himself anymore about the sufferings of our people. Hundreds of thousands fell in the war, not from enemy weapons, but from the hunger blockades. And after the war ended, this blockade was continued for months in order to oppress our people further. Many Germans made prisoners after an endless time had to remain in captivity. The German colonies were stolen from us, Germans' foreign holdings were simply seized and our merchant marine was taken away.

Added to that was a financial plundering such as the world had never before seen. The monetary penalties which were imposed on the German people reached astronomical figures.

On these an English statesman said that they could only be fulfilled when the German standard of living was reduced to the lowest possible level and Germans worked fourteen hours daily.

What German spirit, German alertness, and German labour through decades and decades had accumulated and saved was lost in a few years. Millions of Germans were either torn away from the Reich or were prevented from returning to the Reich. The League of Nations was not an instrument of a just policy of understanding among nations, but it is, and was, a guarantee of the meanest dictation men ever invented.

So was a great people raped and led toward a misery that you all know. A great people through a broken pledge was cheated of its rights, and its existence rendered practically impossible. A French statesman coined the following expression: "There are 20,000,000 Germans too many in the world."

Many Germans ended their lives out of despair. Others slid into lethargy and an inevitable destiny, and still others were of the opinion that everything must be destroyed. Still others set their teeth and clinched their firsts in unconscious rage. Still others believed that the past should be restored—restored just as it was.

Everyone had an idea of some sort. And I, as an unknown soldier of the World War, drew my conclusions. It was a very short and simple programme. It ran—removal of the internal enemies of the nation, termination of the divisions within Germany, the gathering up of the entire national strength of our people into a new community, and the breaking of the peace treaty—in one way or the other.

For as long as this dictate of Versailles weighed upon the German people, it was actually damned to go to the ground. If, however, other statesmen now declare that right must rule on this earth, then they should be told that their criminal dictate is neither right nor law but above this dictate stands the eternal rights of peoples to live. The German people were not created by Providence in order to follow obediently a law which suits the English or the French, but rather in order to champion their right to live. That is why we are here! I was determined to take up this battle of advocating the German right to live. I took it up first within the nation.

In place of a great number of parties, social ranks, and societies, a single community now has taken its place in the German national community! To bring it to realisation and to deepen it more and more is our task. I had to hurt many in this time. However, I believe that the good fortune in which the entire nation is participating today must richly compensate every single one for what he had to give up dearly on his own part.

You all have sacrificed your parties, societies, and associations, but you have obtained in return a great strong Reich. And the Reich today, thank God, is strong enough to take your rights under its protection. We are no longer dependent on the good graces or disgraces of other states or their statesman.

When, more than six years ago, I obtained power, I took over a wretched inheritance. The Reich seemed to possess no more possibilities of existence for its citizens. I undertook the work at that time with the one single capital which I possessed. It was the capital of your strength of work. Your strength to work, my fellow citizens, I now have begun to put to use. I had no foreign exchange. I had no gold reserve. I had only one thing—my faith and your work! Thus we began the gigantic work of rebuilding based upon the confidence of the nation, instilled with the belief and the confidence in its external values.

Now we have found a new economic system, a system which is this: Capital is the power of labour, and coverage of money lies in our production.

We have founded a system based on the most sincere foundation there is, namely: Form your life yourself! Work for your existence! Help yourself and God will help you!

Within a few years we have wrenched Germany from despair. But the work did not help us. If today an English statesman says one can and must solve all problems through frank deliberations, I should like to tell this statesman just this: an opportunity was open for fifteen years before our time.

And one must say: "They did not apply virtuous methods!"

For three hundred years England acted without virtue in order now in maturity to speak of virtue. Thus it would appear that during this British period without virtue, 46,000,000 Englishmen have subdued nearly one-quarter of the world, while 80,000,000 Germans, because of their virtue, must live in a rate of 140 to one square kilometre.

For fifteen years, Germany patiently bore its lot and fate. I also sought in the beginning to solve every problem through tanks, I made an offer in the case of each problem and each time it was turned down!

When today, a British statesman demands that every problem which lies in the midst of Germany's life-interest should first be discussed with England, then I too could demand just as well that every British problem first is to be discussed with us.

Just as we Germans have little to do in Palestine, just as little business has England mixing in our German sector of existence. And if they now declare that it involves general questions of law and justice, I could approve of this opinion only if it was considered as binding on both of us.

Anyway, we have not slaughtered thousands in Central Europe, but instead, we have regulated our problems with law and order.

When the Allies, without regard of purpose, right, tradition, or even reasonableness, changed the map of Europe, we had not the power to prevent it. If, however, they expect the Germany of today to sit patiently until the very last day when this same result would again be repeated — while they create satellite states and set them against Germany — then they are mistaking the Germany of today for the Germany of before the war. He who declares himself ready to pull the chestnuts out of the fire for these powers must realise he burns his fingers.

Really, we feel not hatred against the Czech people. We have lived together for years. The English statesmen do not know this. They have no idea that the Hradschin castle was not built by an Englishman but by a German, and that the St Vitus Cathedral likewise was not erected by Englishmen — German hands did it. Even the French were not active there. They do not know that at a time when England still was very small, a German Kaiser was already paid homage on this hill, Hardcany castle — that one thousand years before me the first German King stood there and accepted the homage of this people.

Despite this, however, we would have had nothing against an independent Czech state if, first, it had not suppressed Germans, and, second, if it had not been intended as the instrument of future attack on Germany. When, however, a former French air minister writes in a newspaper that on the basis of their prominent position it is the task of these Czechs to strike at the heart of German industry with air attacks during war, then one understands that this is not without interest to us and that we draw certain conclusions from it.

It would have been up to England to defend this air base. Upon us fell the task of preventing such an attack at all events. I sought to accomplish this by a natural and simple way.

When I first saw that every effort of that kind was destined to be wrecked and that elements hostile to Germany again would win the upper hand, and as I further saw that this state had long since lost its inner vitality — indeed that it was already broken to pieces — I again carried through the old German Reich. And I joined together again what had to be united by history and geographical positions, and according to all rules of reason. Not to oppress the Czech people! It will enjoy more freedom than the suppressed people of the virtuous nations.

I have, so I believe, thereby rendered peace a great service, because I have rendered innocuous in time an instrument which was destined to become effective in war against Germany. If they now say that this is the signal that Germany now wants to attack the entire world, I do not believe that this is meant seriously: such could only be the expression of a bad conscience. Perhaps it is rage over the failure of some far flung plan; perhaps it is an attempt to create tactical preconditions for a new policy of encirclement.

Be that as it may, it is my conviction that thereby I have rendered peace a great service, and out of conviction I decided three weeks ago to name the coming party rally the Party Convention of Peace.

For German Reich is not only a great producer but also a gigantic consumer. Just as we as a producer will be an irreplaceable trade partner, so as a consumer we are capable of honourably and fairly paying for what we consume.

We are not thinking about making war on other peoples. However, our precondition is that they leave us in peace. In any case, the German Reich is not ready everlastingly to accept intimidation or even a policy of encirclement.

I once made an agreement with England—namely, the Naval Treaty. It is based on the earnest desire which we all possess never to go to war against England. But this wish can only be a mutual one.

If this wish no longer exists in England, then the practical preconditions for this agreement therewith are removed and Germany also would accept this very calmly. We are self-assured because we are strong, and we are strong because we are united and because in addition we are looking forward. And in this city, my fellow citizens, I can address the one exhortation to you: Look into the world and to all its happenings with open eyes. Do not deceive yourself about the most important precondition in life—namely, the necessity to be strong.

We have experienced this for fifteen years. Therefore, I have made Germany strong again and erected an armed force, an army on land, at sea and in the air.

I believe that the time is not far distant in which the philosophical community between Fascist Italy and National Socialist Germany will prove essentially different than the one between democratic Great Britain and the Bolshevist Russia of Stalin. However, if there really should be no ideological differences, then I can only say: How correct, indeed, is my position towards Marxism and communism and democracy! Why the two phenomena if they possess the same contents?

My fellow citizens, I believe that all states will be facing the same problem which we have faced. State after state will either fall under the Jewish-Bolshevist pest or it will defend itself.

We have done it and have now erected a National German People's State. This people's state wants to live in peace and friendship with any other state but it will never again let itself be forced down by another state.

I do not know whether the world would become fascist! But I am deeply convinced that this world in the end will defend itself against the most severe Bolshevistic threat that exists. Therefore I believe that a final understanding between nations will come sooner or later. Only when this Jewish wedge among people is removed can the establishment of cooperation among nations be built on lasting understanding.

Today we must rely upon our own strength! And we can be satisfied with the results of this trust in ourselves — inwardly and outwardly.

Twenty years ago the party was founded — at that time a tiny organisation. Consider the road from the time until today! Consider the wonders which have occurred about us. Believe, therefore, because of this wonderful road, also in the course of the German people in its great future!

Germany — Sieg Heil! Sieg Heil! Sieg Heil!

20. PEREZ DE CUELLAR JAVIER (1920–)

Cuellar is a Peruvian diplomat. He was the UN secretary general from 1982 to 1991.
The following is the speech that he delivered at the UN in Washington in 1991.

*D*uring the past three decades the developing world has made enormous economic progress. This can be seen most clearly in the raising trend for incomes and consumption; between 1965 and 1985 consumption per capita in the developing world went up by almost 70 per cent. Broader measures of well-being confirm this picture – life expectancy, child mortality, and educational attainment have all improved markedly. Viewed from either perspective – income and consumption on the one hand, broad social indicators on the other – the developing countries are advancing much faster than today's developed countries did at a comparable stage.

Against this background of achievement, it is all the more staggering and all the more shameful that more than one billion people in the developing world are living in poverty. World Development Report 1990 estimates that this is the number of people who are struggling to survive on less than $370 a year. Progress in raising average incomes, however welcome, must not distract attention from this massive and continuing burden of poverty.

The same is true of the broader measures of well-being. Life expectancy in Sub-Saharan Africa is just 50 years; in Japan it is almost 80. Mortality among children under five in a South Asia exceeds 170 deaths per thousand; in Sweden it is fewer than 10. More than 110 million children in the developing world lack access even to primary education; in the industrial countries anything less than universal enrollment would rightly be regarded as unacceptable. The starkness of these contrasts attests to the continuing toll of human deprivation.

This report is about poverty in the developing world. In other words, it is concerned with the poorest of the world's poor. It seeks first to measure poverty, qualitatively as well as quantitatively. It then tries to draw lessons for policy from the experience of countries that have succeeded in reducing poverty. It ends with a question that is also a challenge: what might be achieved if governments in rich and poor countries alike made it their goal to attack poverty in this closing decade of the twentieth century?

In the countries that have participated in the overall economic progress that has taken place since the 1960s, poverty has declined and the incomes even of those remaining in poverty have increased. In some cases this change has been dramatic. Indonesia, for example, took less than a generation in the 1970s and 1980s to reduce the incidence of poverty from almost 60 per cent of the population to less than 20 per cent. On a variety of social indicators, some developing countries are now approaching the standards of the developed world. In China, which accounts for a quarter of the developing world's people, life expectancy reached 69 in 1985, but in many countries economic performance was weaker, and the number in poverty fell more slowly. Where rapid population growth was an important additional factor, as in much of sub-Saharan Africa, consumption per head stagnated and the number in poverty rose.

The 1980s — often called a "lost decade" for the poor — did not, in fact, reverse the overall trend of progress. The incomes of most of the world's poor went on rising, and under five mortality, primary school enrolment ratios; and other social indicators also continued to improve. The setback of the 1980s fell heavily on particular regions. For many in sub-Saharan Africa and Latin America, incomes fell during the decade and the incidence of poverty increased — although the social indicators, at least in Latin America, proved somewhat more resilient.

The burden of poverty is spread unevenly — among the regions of the developing world, among countries within those regions, and among localities within those countries. Nearly half of the world's poor live in South Asia, a region that accounts for roughly 30 percent of the world's population. Sub-Saharan Africa accounts for a smaller, but still highly disproportionate, share of global poverty. Within regions and countries, the poor are often concentrated in certain places in rural areas with high population densities, such as the Gangetic Plains of India and the islands of Java, Indonesia, or in resource-poor areas such as the Andean highlands and the Sahel. Often the problems of poverty, population, and the environment are intertwined: earlier patterns of development and the pressure of rapidly expanding population mean that many of the poor live in areas of acute environmental degradation.

The weight of poverty falls most heavily on certain groups. Women in general are disadvantaged. In poor households they often shoulder more of the workload than men, are less educated, and have less access to remunerative activities. Children, too, suffer disproportionately, and the future quality of their lives in compromised by inadequate nutrition, health care, and education. This is especially true for girls: their primary enrolment rates are less than 50 per cent in many African countries. The incidence of poverty is often high among ethnic groups and minorities such as the indigenous peoples in Bolivia, Ecuador, Guatemala, Mexico, and Peru and the scheduled castes in India.

In many but not all cases low incomes go hand in hand with other forms of deprivation. In Mexico, for example, life expectancy for the poorest 10 per cent of the population is twenty year less than for the richest 10 per cent. In Cote D' Ivorie the primary enrolment rate of the poorest fifth is half that of the richest. National and regional averages, often bad enough in themselves, mask appalling low life expectancy and educational attainment among the poorest members of society.

In the 1950s and 1960s many saw growth as the primary means for reducing poverty and improving the quality of life. For example, the Indian Planning Commission viewed rapid growth as the main (although not the only) instrument for achieving this objective. In the 1970s attention shifted to the direct provision of health, nutritional, and educational services. This was seen as a matter of public policy. World Development Report 1980, marshaling the evidence available at the time, argued that improvements in the health, education, and nutrition of the poor were important not only in their own right but also to promote growth in incomes, including the incomes of the poor.

The 1980s saw another shift in emphasis. Countries, especially in Latin America and sub-Saharan Africa, struggled to adjust after the global recession. The constraints on public spending tightened. At the same time, many began to question the effectiveness of public policy, and especially policy toward the poor. Against this background, World Development Report 1990 re-examines how policy can help to reduce poverty and explore the prospects for the poor during the 1990s.

The evidence in this report suggests that rapid and politically sustainable progress on poverty has been achieved by pursuing a strategy that has two equally important elements. The first element is to promote the productive use of the poor's most abundant asset—labour. It calls for policies that harness market incentives, social and political institutions, infrastructure, and technology to that end. The second is to provide basic social services to the poor. Primary health care, family planning nutrition, and primary education are especially important.

The two elements are mutually reinforcing; one without the other is not sufficient. In some countries, such as Brazil and Pakistan, growth has raised the incomes of the poor, but social services have received too little attention. As a result, mortality among children remains usually high and primary enrolment usually low, and the poor are not as well equipped as they might be to take advantage of economic opportunities. Some other countries, by contrast, have long stressed the provision of social services, but growth has been too slow. In Sri Lanka, for example, primary enrolment.

Even if this basic two-part strategy is adopted, many of the world's poor—the sick, the old, those who live in resource-poor regions, and others—will continue to experience severe deprivation. Many others will suffer temporary setbacks owing to seasonal variations in income, loss of the family breadwinner, famine, or adverse macroeconomic shocks. A comprehensive approach to poverty reduction, therefore, calls for a programme of well-targeted transfers and safety nets as an essential complement to the basic strategy.

During the 1980s many developing countries had to cope with macroeconomic crises. Their experience drew attention to a new concern: the need to frame adjustment policies that give due weight to the need of the poor. In many developing countries a period of painful macroeconomic adjustment was unavoidable. In the longer term the economic restructuring associated with adjustment is perfectly consistent with the two-part strategy. In the short term, however, many of the poor are at risk. During the transition period the poor can be protected through a judicious mix of macroeconomic policies—for example, pricing policy reforms that benefit poor farmers—and measures to moderate declines in private consumption. Experience also shows that it is possible to shift public spending in favour of the poor, even within an overall framework of fiscal discipline, and to target transfers more accurately. In addition, increased capital inflows can be used to help cushion the impact of adjustment among the poor.

The framework of political and economic institutions is important because policies to reduce poverty involve a tradeoff. This tradeoff is not, in the main, between growth and the reduction of poverty. Switching to an efficient, labour-intensive pattern of development and investing more in the human capital of the poor are not only consistent with faster long-term growth; they contribute to it. Since these actions mean that a larger share of income and more public spending will go to the poor, the principal tradeoff, especially in the short run, is between the interests of the poor and those of the non-poor. The two-part strategy is, therefore more likely to be adopted in countries where the poor have a say in political and economic decision-making.

Although the two-part strategy does involve a politically sensitive tradeoff between the poor and the non-poor, it is likely to prove more feasible than other strategies. Large-scale redistributions of land have sometimes been successful. In Japan and the Republic of Korea, for example, land redistribution was central to the reduction of rural poverty and laid the basis for the other policies advocated in this report. Where it can be done, redistribution of land should be strongly supported. But the political obstacles to such reform are great. In most countries the two-part strategy outlined here, which sees investment in education as the best way of augmenting the assets of the poor, is more likely to succeed.

Even when macroeconomic adjustment is not a primary issue, the strategy requires an increase in certain categories of public spending that specifically benefit the poor. If these are to be affordable and hence sustainable, they must be cost-effective.

Experience since the 1970s shows, however, that reaching the poor with targeted programmes can be difficult. Nongovernmental organizations have made important contributions here. Self-selecting programmes, which exclude the non-poor by offering benefits that are of interests only to the poor, are another promising approach. Low-wage public employment programmes, for instance, have provided an effective safety net for the poor in certain parts of South Asia and have been especially valuable in preventing famine. Chile's experience suggests that such schemes may also be helpful during recessions.

To be truly cost-effective, interventions must be not merely well targeted but also carefully designed to meet the specific needs of the poor people. This means developing technologies suited to the risky environment that confronts small farmers, devising credit schemes to serve small borrowers, combining feeding programmes for especially vulnerable groups with education on health and nutrition, and so on. Successful programmes have usually involved the poor both at the design stage and during implementation.

Public spending that is well designed and accurately targeted can play an important part in the fight against poverty. But such programmes, however cost-effective, are no substitute for efforts to attune the broad stance of economic policy to the needs of the poor. Attacking poverty is not primarily a task for narrowly focused antipoverty projects, vital though these may be. It is a task for economic policy on the large.

Aid has often been an effective instrument for reducing poverty – but not always. Donors sometimes have other objectives. In 1988 about 41 per cent of external assistance was directed to middle and high-income countries, largely for political reasons. Even when aid has been directed to the poor, the results have sometimes been disappointing – especially in countries in which the overall policy framework has not been conducive to the reduction of poverty.

The world is at a turning point: the geopolitical tensions that have prevailed since World War II are easing rapidly. This offers a unique opportunity to cut military spending and increase international assistance. A cut of just 10 per cent in military spending by the countries of the North Atlantic Treaty Organisation would pay for a doubling aid. The resource can be made available; though little will be achieved unless they are used effectively.

The analysis in this report provides the basis for a better aid strategy. External assistance should be more tightly linked to an assessment of the efforts that would-be recipients are making to reduce poverty. This principle already underlies procedures for allocating the resources of the International Development Association (IDA). Carrying out this principle would mean that countries committed to the two-part strategy would be the main recipients of aid. This reflects the conviction that aid works well only when it complements a sound development strategy.

In countries where policies — on prices and public spending, for instance — are inconsistent with efforts to reduce poverty, external resources would achieve far less. Yet there are many poor people in such countries. Indeed, these are the very countries in which poverty is going to get worse. The judgements that have to be made in such cases will be extremely difficult. Aiming moderate quantities of aid directly at highly vulnerable groups seems the appropriate response. Health clinics that serve the poor, immunization programmes for children, and targeted nutrition programmes are the sorts for intervention that might be supported by the aid community in such circumstances.

Many countries will fall between these two extremes. In such cases, intermediate amounts of assistance would be appropriate. Careful judgement is needed to determine how this aid can best be used to make policy more responsive to the needs of the poor.

These principles certainly bear on the operations of the World Bank, but they should be regarded as applicable to the aid of community as a whole. If the aid strategy outlined here were adopted and followed consistently by bilateral donors, nongovernment organizations, and multinational agencies, its effectiveness would be greatly increased.

21. THOMAS JEFFERSON (1743–1826)

Thomas Jefferson, the third American president (1801–1809), was the author of the Declaration of Independence, *and a preeminent spokesman for human liberty.*
This is the first inaugural speech he gave as the president of the US.

Ƒ riends and fellow citizens:
Called upon to undertake the duties of the first executive office of our country, I avail myself of the presence of that portion of my fellow-citizens which is here assembled to express my grateful thanks for the favour with which they have been pleased to look towards me, to declare a sincere consciousness that the task is above my talents, and that I approach it with those anxious awful presentiments, which the greatness of the charge and weakness of my powers so justly inspire.

A rising nation, spread over a wide and fruitful land, traversing all the seas with the rich productions of their industry, engaged in commerce with nations who feel power and forget right, advancing rapidly to destinies beyond the reach of mortal eye — when I contemplate these transcendent objects, and see the honour, the happiness and the hopes of this beloved country committed to the issue and the auspices of this day, I shrink from the contemplation, and humble myself before the magnitude of the undertaking.

During the contest of opinion through which we have passed, the animation of discussions and of exertions has sometimes worn an aspect which might impose on strangers unused to think freely and to speak and to write what they think; but this being now decided by the voice of the nation, announced according to the rules of the constitution, all will, of course, arrange themselves under the will of the law, and unite in common efforts for the common good. All, too, will bear in mind this sacred principle, that though the will of the majority is in all cases to prevail, that will be rightful, must be reasonable, that the minority possess their equal rights which equal law must protect, and to violate would be oppression.

Let us, then, fellow citizens, unite with one heart and one mind. Let us restore to social intercourse that harmony and affection without which liberty and even life itself are but dreary things.

And let us reflect that, having banished from our land that religious intolerance under which mankind so long bled and suffered, we have yet gained little if we countenance a political intolerance as despotic, as wicked and capable of as bitter and bloody persecutions.

During the throes and convulsions of the ancient world, during the agonising spasms of infuriated man, seeking through blood and slaughter his long-lost liberty, it was not wonderful that the agitation of the billows should reach even this distant and peaceful shore; that this should be more felt and feared by some and less by others, and should divide opinions as to measures of safety. But every difference of opinion is not a difference of principle. We have called by different names brethren of the same principle. We are all Republicans, we are all Federalists.

If there be any among us who would wish to dissolve this union or to change its republican form, let them stand undisturbed as monuments of the safety with which error of opinion may be tolerated where reason is left free to combat it.

I know, indeed, that some honest men fear that a Republican government cannot be strong, that this government is not strong enough; but would the honest patriot, in the full tide of successful experiment, abandon a government which has so far kept us free and firm on the theoretic and visionary fear that this government, the world's best hope, may by possibility want energy to preserve itself?

I trust not I believe this, on the contrary; the strongest government on earth, I believe, is the only one where every man, at the call of the law, would fly to the standard of the law, and would meet invasions of the public order as his own personal concern. Sometimes it is said that man cannot be trusted with the government of others. Or have we found angels in the forms of kings to govern him? Oh, let history answer these questions.

Let us, then, with courage and confidence pursue our own
Federal and Republican principles, our attachment to union and
representative goverr.ment. Kindly separated by nature and a
wide ocean from the exterminating havoc of one quarter of the
globe; too high-minded to endure the degradations of the others;
possessing a chosen country, with room enough for our
descendants to the thousandth and thousandth generation;
entertaining a due sense of our equal right to the use of our own
faculties, to the acquisitions of our own industry, to honour and
confidence from our fellow citizens, resulting not from birth, but
from our actions and their sense of them; enlightened by a benign
religion, professed, indeed, and practised, in various forms, yet
all of them inculcating honesty, truth, temperance, gratitude and
the love of men; acknowledging and adoring an overruling
Providence which by all its dispensations proves that it delights
in the happiness of man here and his greater happiness hereafter.
With all these blessings, what more is necessary to make us a
happy and a prosperous people?

Still one thing more, fellow-citizens, a wise and frugal
government, which shall restrain men from injuring one another,
shall leave them otherwise free to regulate their own pursuits of
industry and improvement and shall not take from the mouth of
labour, the bread it has earned. This is the sum of good
government, and this is necessary to close the circle of our
felicities.

I repair, then, fellow-citizens to the post you have assigned
me with experience enough in subordinate offices to have seen
the difficulties of this the greatest of all, I have learnt to expect
that it will rarely fall to the lot of imperfect man to retire from
this station with the reputation and the favour which bring him
into it.

Without pretensions to that high confidence you respond in
our first and greatest revolutionary character, whose preeminent
services had entitled him to the first place in his country's love
and destined for him the fairest page in the volume of faithful
history, I ask so much confidence only as may give firmness and
effect to the legal administration of your affairs.

I shall often go wrong through defect of judgement when
right. I shall often be though wrong by those whose positions
will not command a view of the whole ground. I ask your

indulgence for my own errors, which will never be intentional and your support against the errors of others who may condemn what they would not if seen in all its parts. The approbation implied by your suffrage is a great consolation to me for the past, and my future solicitude will be to retain the good opinion of those who have bestowed it in advance, to conciliate that of others by doing them all the good in my power and to be instrumental to the happiness and freedom of all.

Relying then on the patronage of your goodwill, I advance with obedience to the work, ready to retire from it whenever you become sensible how much better choice it is in your power to make. And may that infinite Power, which rules the destinies of the universe, lead our councils to what is best, give them favourable issue for your peace and prosperity.

22. LYNDON B JOHNSON (1908–1973)

*Lyndon Baines Johnson was the US president from 1963 to 1969.
The following is his address to the nation on 31 March 1968,
announcing steps to limit the war in Vietnam, and reporting his
decision not to seek reelection.*

*T*onight I want to speak to you of peace in Vietnam and
Southeast Asia.

No other question so preoccupies our people. No other dream
so absorbs the 250 million human beings who live in that part of
the world. No other goal motivates American policy in Southeast
Asia.

For years, representatives of our government and others have
traveled the world — seeking to find a basis for peace talks. Since
last September, they have carried the offer that I made public at
San Antonio. That offer was this: That the United States would
stop its bombardment of North Vietnam when that would lead
promptly to productive discussions — and that we would assume
that North Vietnam would not take military advantage of our
restraint. Hanoi denounced this offer, both privately and publicly.
Even while the search for peace was going on, North Vietnam
rushed their preparations for a savage assault on the people, the
government, and the allies of South Vietnam.

Their attack — during the Tet holidays — failed to achieve its
principal objectives.

It did not collapse the elected government of South Vietnam
or shatter its army — as the communists had hoped. It did not
produce a "general uprising" among the people of the cities as
they had predicted. The communists were unable to maintain
control of any of the more than 30 cities that they attacked. And
they took very heavy casualties. But they did compel the South
Vietnamese and their allies to move certain forces from the

countryside into the cities. They caused widespread disruption and suffering. Their attacks, and the battles that followed, made refugees of half a million human beings.

The communists may renew their attack any day. They are, it appears, trying to make 1968 the year of decision in South Vietnam—the year that brings, if not final victory or defeat, at least a turning point in the struggle.

This much is clear: If they do mount another round of heavy attacks, they will not succeed in destroying the fighting power of South Vietnam and its allies. But tragically, this is also clear: Many men—on both sides of the struggle—will be lost. A nation that has already suffered 20 years of warfare will suffer once again. Armies on both sides will take new casualties. And the war will go on. There is no need for this to be so. There is no need to delay the talks that could bring an end to this long and this bloody war.

Tonight, I renew the offer I made last August—to stop the bombardment of North Vietnam. We ask that talks begin promptly, that they be serious talks on the substance of peace. We assume that during those talks Hanoi will not take advantage of our restraint. We are prepared to move immediately toward peace through negotiations. So, tonight, in the hope that this action will lead to early talks, I am taking the first step to de-escalate the conflict. We are reducing—substantially reducing—the present level of hostilities. And we are doing so unilaterally, and at once.

Tonight, I have ordered our aircraft and our naval vessels to make no attacks on North Vietnam, except in the area north of the demilitarized zone where the continuing enemy buildup directly threatens allied forward positions and where the movements of their troops and supplies are clearly related to that threat. The area in which we are stopping our attacks includes almost 90 percent of North Vietnam's population, and most of its territory. Thus there will be no attacks around the principal populated areas, or in the food-producing areas of North Vietnam.

Even this very limited bombing of the North could come to an early end—if our restraint is matched by restraint in Hanoi. But I cannot in good conscience stop all bombing so long as to do so would immediately and directly endanger the lives of our men and our allies. Whether a complete bombing halt becomes possible in the future will be determined by events. Our purpose in this action is to bring about a reduction in the level of violence that now exists. It is to save the lives of brave men—and to save the lives of innocent women and children. It is to permit the contending forces to move closer to a political settlement.

And tonight, I call upon the United Kingdom and I call upon the Soviet Union—as cochairmen of the Geneva Conferences, and as permanent members of the United Nations Security Council—to do all they can to move from the unilateral act of de-escalation that I have just announced toward genuine peace in Southeast Asia.

Now, as in the past, the United States is ready to send its representatives to any forum, at any time, to discuss the means of bringing this ugly war to an end.

I am designating one of our most distinguished Americans, Ambassador Averell Harriman, as my personal representative for such talks. In addition, I have asked Ambassador Llewellyn Thompson, who returned from Moscow for consultation, to be available to join Ambassador Harriman at Geneva or any other suitable place—just as soon as Hanoi agrees to a conference.

I call upon President Ho Chi Minh to respond positively, and favourably, to this new step toward peace. But if peace does not come now through negotiations, it will come when Hanoi understands that our common resolve is unshakable, and our common strength is invincible. Tonight, we and the other allied nations are contributing 600,000 fighting men to assist 700,000 South Vietnamese troops in defending their little country. Our presence there has always rested on this basic belief: The main burden of preserving their freedom must be carried out by them—by the South Vietnamese themselves. We and our allies can only help to provide a shield behind which the people of South Vietnam can survive and can grow and develop. On their efforts—on their determination and resourcefulness—the outcome will ultimately depend. That small, beleaguered nation has suffered terrible punishment for more than 20 years.

I pay tribute once again tonight to the great courage and endurance of its people. South Vietnam supports armed forces tonight of almost 700,000 men—and I call your attention to the fact that this is the equivalent of more than 10 million in our own population. Its people maintain their firm determination to be free of domination by the North. There has been substantial progress, I think, in building a durable government during these last 3 years. The South Vietnam of 1965 could not have survived the enemy's Tet offensive of 1968. The elected government of South Vietnam survived that attack—and is rapidly repairing the devastation that it wrought.

The South Vietnamese know that further efforts are going to be required:

- to expand their own armed forces,
- to move back into the countryside as quickly as possible,
- to increase their taxes,
- to select the very best men that they have for civil and military responsibility,
- to achieve a new unity within their constitutional government, and
- to include in the national effort all those groups who wish to preserve South Vietnam's control over its own destiny.

Last week President Thieu ordered the mobilisation of 135,000 additional South Vietnamese. He plans to reach, as soon as possible, a total military strength of more than 800,000 men. To achieve this, the government of South Vietnam started the drafting of 19-year-olds on March 1st. On May 1st, the Government will begin the drafting of 18-year-olds.

Last month, 10,000 men volunteered for military service—that was two and a half times the number of volunteers during the same month last year. Since the middle of January, more than 48,000 South Vietnamese have joined the armed forces, and nearly half of them volunteered to do so. All men in the South Vietnamese armed forces have had their tours of duty extended for the duration of the war, and reserves are now being called-up for immediate active duty.

President Thieu told his people last week: "We must make greater efforts and accept more sacrifices because, as I have said many times, this is our country. The existence of our nation is at stake, and this is mainly a Vietnamese responsibility." He warned his people that a major national effort is required to root out corruption and incompetence at all levels of government. We applaud this evidence of determination on the part of South Vietnam. Our first priority will be to support their effort. We shall accelerate the reequipment of South Vietnam's armed forces, in order to meet the enemy's increased firepower. This will enable them progressively to undertake a larger share of combat operations against the Communist invaders.

On many occasions I have told the American people that we would send to Vietnam those forces that are required to accomplish our mission there. So, with that as our guide, we have previously authorised a force level of approximately 525,000. Some weeks ago — to help meet the enemy's new offensive — we sent to Vietnam about 11,000 additional marine and airborne troops. They were deployed by air in 48 hours, on an emergency basis. But the artillery, tank, aircraft, medical, and other units that were needed to work with and to support these infantry troops in combat could not then accompany them by air on that short notice.

In order that these forces may reach maximum combat effectiveness, the Joint Chiefs of Staff have recommended to me that we should prepare to send during the next 5 months support troops totaling approximately 13,500 men. A portion of these men will be made available from our active forces. The balance will come from reserve component units which will be called up for service.

The actions that we have taken since the beginning of the year:
  — to reequip the South Vietnamese forces,
  — to meet our responsibilities in Korea, as well as our responsibilities in Vietnam,
  — to meet price increases and the cost of activating and deploying reserve forces,
  — to replace helicopters and provide the other military supplies we need. All of these actions are going to require additional expenditures.

The tentative estimate of those additional expenditures is $2.5 billion in this fiscal year, and $2.6 billion in the next fiscal year.

These projected increases in expenditures for our national security will bring into sharper focus the nation's need for immediate action — action to protect the prosperity of the American people and to protect the strength and the stability of our American dollar.

On many occasions I have pointed out that, without a tax bill or decreased expenditures, next year's deficit would again be around $20 billion. I have emphasized the need to set strict priorities in our spending. I have stressed that failure to act, and to act promptly and decisively, would raise very strong doubts throughout the world about America's willingness to keep its financial house in order. Yet, Congress has not acted. And tonight we face the sharpest financial threat in the postwar era — a threat to the dollar's role as the keystone of international trade and finance in the world.

Last week, at the monetary conference in Stockholm, the major industrial countries decided to take a big step toward creating a new international monetary asset that will strengthen the international monetary system. I am very proud of the very able work done by Secretary Fowler and Chairman Martin of the Federal Reserve Board.

But to make this system work the United States just must bring its balance of payments to — or very close to — equilibrium. We must have a responsible fiscal policy in this country. The passage of a tax bill now, together with expenditure control that the Congress may desire and dictate, is absolutely necessary to protect this nation's security, to continue our prosperity, and to meet the needs of our people. What is at stake is seven years of unparalleled prosperity. In those seven years, the real income of the average American, after taxes, rose by almost 30 per cent — a gain as large as that of the entire preceding 19 years. So the steps that we must take to convince the world are exactly the steps we must take to sustain our own economic strength here at home. In the past 8 months, prices and interest rates have risen because of our inaction. We must, therefore, now do everything we can to move from debate to action — from talking to voting. There is, I believe — I hope there is — in both Houses of the Congress, a growing sense of urgency that this situation just must be acted upon and must be corrected.

My budget in January was, we thought, a tight one. It fully reflected our evaluation of most of the demanding needs of this nation. But in these budgetary matters, the president does not decide alone. The Congress has the power and the duty to determine appropriations and taxes. The Congress is now considering our proposals and they are considering reductions in the budget that we submitted. As part of a programme of fiscal restraint that includes the tax surcharge, I shall approve appropriate reductions in the January budget when and if Congress so decides that that should be done.

One thing is unmistakably clear, however. Our deficit just must be reduced. Failure to act could bring on conditions that would strike hardest at those people that all of us are trying so hard to help. These times call for prudence in this land of plenty. I believe that we have the character to provide it, and tonight I plead with the Congress and with the people to act promptly to serve the national interest, and thereby serve all of our people.

Now let me give you my estimate of the chances for peace:
 — the peace that will one day stop the bloodshed in South Vietnam,
 — that will permit all the Vietnamese people to rebuild and develop their land,
 — that will permit us to turn more fully to our own tasks here at home.

I cannot promise that the initiative that I have announced tonight will be completely successful in achieving peace any more than the 30 others that we have undertaken and agreed to in recent years. But it is our fervent hope that North Vietnam, after years of fighting that have left the issue unresolved, will now cease its efforts to achieve a military victory and will join with us in moving toward the peace table. And there may come a time when South Vietnamese — on both sides — are able to work out a way to settle their own differences by free political choice rather than by war.

As Hanoi considers its course, it should be in no doubt of our intentions. It must not miscalculate the pressures within our democracy in this election year. We have no intention of widening this war. But the United States will never accept a fake solution to this long and arduous struggle and call it peace. No one can foretell the precise terms of an eventual settlement. Our objective in South Vietnam has never been the annihilation of the enemy. It has been to bring about a recognition in Hanoi that its objective — taking over the South by force — could not be achieved. We think that peace can be based on the Geneva Accords of 1954, under political conditions that permit the South Vietnamese — all the South Vietnamese — to chart their course free of any outside domination or interference, from us or from anyone else.

So tonight I reaffirm the pledge that we made at Manila — that we are prepared to withdraw our forces from South Vietnam as the other side withdraws its forces to the North, stops the infiltration, and the level of violence thus subsides. Our goal of peace and self-determination in Vietnam is directly related to the future of all of Southeast Asia—where much has happened to inspire confidence during the past 10 years. We have done all that we knew how to do to contribute and to help build that confidence.

A number of its nations have shown what can be accomplished under conditions of security. Since 1966, Indonesia, the fifth largest nation in all the world, with a population of more than 100 million people, has had a government that is dedicated to peace with its neighbours and improved conditions for its own people. Political and economic cooperation between nations has grown rapidly.

I think every American can take a great deal of pride in the role that we have played in bringing this about in Southeast Asia. We can rightly judge—as responsible Southeast Asians themselves do—that the progress of the past three years would have been far less likely, if not completely impossible, if America's sons and others had not made their stand in Vietnam.

At Johns Hopkins University, about three years ago, I announced that the United States would take part in the great work of developing Southeast Asia, including the Mekong Valley, for all the people of that region. Our determination to help build a better land—a better land for men on both sides of the present conflict—has not diminished in the least. Indeed, the ravages of war, I think, have made it more urgent than ever. So, I repeat on behalf of the United States again tonight what I said at Johns Hopkins—that North Vietnam could take its place in this common effort just as soon as peace comes.

Over time, a wider framework of peace and security in Southeast Asia may become possible. The new cooperation of the nations of the area could be a foundation-stone. Certainly friendship with the nations of such a Southeast Asia is what the United States seeks—and that is all that the United States seeks.

One day, my fellow citizens, there will be peace in Southeast Asia. It will come because the people of Southeast Asia want it. Those whose armies are at war tonight, and those who, though threatened, have thus far been spared. Peace will come because Asians were willing to work for it, and to sacrifice for it, and to die by the thousands for it. But let it never be forgotten: Peace will come also because America sent her sons to help secure it.

It has not been easy. Far from it. During the past four and a half years, it has been my fate and my responsibility to be commander-in- chief. I have lived—daily and nightly—with the cost of this war. I know the pain that it has inflicted. I know, perhaps better than anyone, the misgivings that it has aroused. Throughout this entire, long period, I have been sustained by a single principle: that what we are doing now, in Vietnam, is vital not only to the security of Southeast Asia, but it is vital to the security of every American. Surely we have treaties which we must respect. Surely we have commitments that we are going to keep. Resolutions of the Congress testif·' to the need to resist aggression in the world and in Southeast Asia.

But the heart of our involvement in South Vietnam—under three different presidents, three separate administrations—has always been America's own security. And the larger purpose of our involvement has always been to help the nations of Southeast Asia become independent and stand alone, self-sustaining, as members of a great world community—at peace with themselves, and at peace with all others. With such an Asia, our country—and the world—will be far more secure than it is tonight.

I believe that a peaceful Asia is far nearer to reality because of what America has done in Vietnam. I believe that the men who endure the dangers of battle—fighting there for us tonight—are helping the entire world avoid far greater conflicts, far wider wars, far more destruction, than this one. The peace that will bring them home someday will come. Tonight I have offered the first in what I hope will be a series of mutual moves toward peace.

I pray that it will not be rejected by the leaders of North Vietnam. I pray that they will accept it as a means by which the sacrifices of their own people may be ended. And I ask your help and your support, my fellow citizens, for this effort to reach across the battlefield toward an early peace.

Finally, my fellow Americans, let me say this: Of those to whom much is given, much is asked. I cannot say and no man could say that no more will be asked of us. Yet, I believe that now, no less than when the decade began, this generation of Americans is willing to pay any price, bear any burden, meet any hardship, support any friend, oppose any foe to assure the survival and the success of liberty. Since those words were spoken by

John F Kennedy, the people of America have kept that compact with mankind's noblest cause. And we shall continue to keep it. Yet, I believe that we must always be mindful of this one thing: whatever the trials and the tests ahead, the ultimate strength of our country and our cause will lie not in powerful weapons or infinite resources or boundless wealth, but will lie in the unity of our people. This I believe very deeply.

Throughout my entire public career I have followed the personal philosophy that I am a free man, an American, a public servant, and a member of my party, in that order always and only. For 37 years in the service of our nation, first as a Congressman, as a Senator, and as Vice President, and now as your President, I have put the unity of the people first. I have put it ahead of any divisive partisanship. And in these times as in times before, it is true that a house divided against itself by the spirit of faction, of party, of region, of religion, of race, is a house that cannot stand.

There is division in the American house now. There is divisiveness among us all tonight. And holding the trust that is mine, as President of all the people, I cannot disregard the peril to the progress of the American people and the hope and the prospect of peace for all peoples. So, I would ask all Americans, whatever their personal interests or concern, to guard against divisiveness and all its ugly consequences.

Fifty-two months and 10 days ago, in a moment of tragedy and trauma, the duties of this office fell upon me. I asked then for your help and God's, that we might continue America on its course, binding up our wounds, healing our history, moving forward in new unity, to clear the American agenda and to keep the American commitment for all of our people. United we have kept that commitment. United we have enlarged that commitment. Through all time to come, I think America will be a stronger nation, a more just society, and a land of greater opportunity and fulfillment because of what we have all done together in these years of unparalleled achievement. Our reward will come in the life of freedom, peace, and hope that our children will enjoy through ages ahead. What we won when all of our people united just must not now be lost in suspicion, distrust, selfishness, and politics among any of our people. Believing this as I do, I have concluded that I should not permit the presidency to become involved in the partisan divisions that are developing in this political year.

With America's sons in the fields far away, with America's future under challenge right here at home, with our hopes and the world's hopes for peace in the balance every day, I do not believe that I should devote an hour or a day of my time to any personal partisan causes or to any duties other than the awesome duties of this office—the presidency of your country. Accordingly, I shall not seek, and I will not accept, the nomination of my party for another term as your president. But let men everywhere know, however, that a strong, a confident, and a vigilant America stands ready tonight to seek an honourable peace—and stands ready tonight to defend an honoured cause—whatever the price, whatever the burden, whatever the sacrifice that duty may require.

Thank you for listening. Good night and God bless all of you.

23. EDWARD KENNEDY (1932–)

*Edward Kennedy is the younger brother of the late US president,
John F Kennedy. He is a senior senator from Massachusetts in the
US.*

*He delivered the following speech on the Iraq war and preemptive
talks on 7 October 2002 in Washington.*

*W*e face no more serious decision in our democracy than
whether or not to go to war. The American people deserve
to fully understand all of the implications of such a decision. The
question of whether our nation should attack Iraq is playing out
in the context of a more fundamental debate that is only just
beginning an all-important debate about how, when and where
in the years ahead our country will use its unsurpassed military
might.

On September 20, the Administration unveiled its new
National Security Strategy. This document addresses the new
realities of our age, particularly, the proliferation of weapons of
mass destruction and terrorist networks armed with the agendas
of fanatics. The Strategy claims that these new threats are so
novel and so dangerous that we should "not hesitate to act alone,
if necessary, to exercise our right of self-defence by acting
preemptively."

But in the discussion over the past few months about Iraq,
the Administration, often uses the terms "preemptive" and
"preventive" interchangeably. In the realm of international
relations, these two terms have long had very different meanings.

Traditionally, "preemptive" action refers to times when states
react to an imminent threat of attack. For example, when Egyptian
and Syrian forces mobilised on Israel's borders in 1967, the threat
was obvious and immediate, and Israel felt justified in

preemptively attacking those forces. The global community is generally tolerant of such actions, since no nation should have to suffer a certain first strike before it has the legitimacy to respond.

By contrast, "preventive" military action refers to strikes that target a country before it has developed a capability that could someday become threatening. Preventive attacks have generally been condemned. For example, the 1941 sneak attack on Pearl Harbour was regarded as a preventive strike by Japan because the Japanese were seeking to block a planned military buildup by the United States in the Pacific. The coldly premeditated nature of preventive attacks and preventive wars makes them anathema to well-established international principles against aggression. Pearl Harbor has been rightfully recorded in history as an act of dishonourable treachery.

Historically, the United States has condemned the idea of preventive war because it violates basic international rules against aggression. But at times in our history, preventive war has been seriously advocated as a policy option.

In the early days of the Cold War, some US military and civilian experts advocated a preventive war against the Soviet Union. They proposed a devastating first strike to prevent the Soviet Union from developing a threatening nuclear capability. At the time, they said the uniquely destructive power of nuclear weapons required us to rethink traditional international rules.

The first round of that debate ended in 1950, when President Truman ruled out a preventive strike, stating that such actions were not consistent with our American tradition. He said, "You don't 'prevent' anything by war...except peace." Instead of a surprise first strike, the nation dedicated itself to the strategy of deterrence and containment, which successfully kept the peace during the long and frequently difficult years of the Cold War.

Arguments for preventive war resurfaced again when the Eisenhower Administration took power in 1953, but President Eisenhower and Secretary of State John Foster Dulles soon decided firmly against it. President Eisenhower emphasized that even if we were to win such a war, we would face the vast burdens of occupation and reconstruction that would come with it. The argument that the United States should take preventive military action, in the absence of an imminent attack, resurfaced in 1962, when we learned that the Soviet Union would soon have the ability to launch missiles from Cuba against our country. Many military officers urged President Kennedy to approve a preventive attack to destroy this capability before it became operational. Robert Kennedy, like Harry Truman, felt that this kind of first strike was not consistent with American values. He said that a proposed surprise first strike against Cuba would be a Pearl Harbor in reverse. "For 175 years," he said, "we have not been that kind of country." That view prevailed. A middle ground was found and peace was preserved.

Yet another round of debate followed the Cuban Missile Crisis when American strategists and voices in and out of the Administration advocated preventive war against China to forestall its acquisition of nuclear weapons. Many arguments heard today about Iraq were made then about the Chinese communist government: that its leadership was irrational and that it was therefore undeterrable. And once again, those arguments were rejected.

As these earlier cases show, American strategic thinkers have long debated the relative merits of preventive and preemptive war. Although nobody would deny our right to preemptively block an imminent attack on our territory, there is disagreement about our right to preventively engage in war. In each of these cases, a way was found to deter other nations, without waging war. Now, the Bush Administration says we must take preemptive action against Iraq. But what the Administration is really calling for is preventive war, which flies in the face of international rules of acceptable behaviour. The Administration's new National Security Strategy states: As a matter of common sense and self-defense, America will act against such emerging threats before they are fully formed.

The circumstances of today's world require us to rethink this concept. The world changed on September 11th, and all of us have learned that it can be a drastically more dangerous place. The Bush Administration's new National Security Strategy asserts that global realities now legitimise preventive war and make it a strategic necessity. The document openly contemplates preventive attacks against groups or states, even absent the threat of imminent attack. It legitimises this kind of first strike option, and it elevates it to the status of a core security doctrine. Disregarding norms of international behavior, the Bush strategy asserts that the United States should be exempt from the rules we expect other nations to obey.

I strongly oppose any such extreme doctrine and I'm sure that many others do as well. Earlier generations of Americans rejected preventive war on the grounds of both morality and practicality, and our generation must do so as well. We can deal with Iraq without resorting to this extreme. It is impossible to justify any such double standard under international law. Might does not make right. America cannot write its own rules for the modern world. To attempt to do so would be unilateralism run amok. It would antagonise our closest allies, whose support we need to fight terrorism, prevent global warming, and deal with many other dangers that affect all nations and require international cooperation. It would deprive America of the moral legitimacy necessary to promote our values abroad. And it would give other nations — from Russia to India to Pakistan — an excuse to violate fundamental principles of civilised international behaviour.

The Administration's doctrine is a call for twenty-first century American imperialism that no other nation can or should accept. It is the antithesis of all that America has worked so hard to achieve in international relations since the end of World War II. This is not just an academic debate. There are important real world consequences. A shift in our policy toward preventive war would reinforce the perception of America as a "bully" in the Middle East, and would fuel anti-American sentiment throughout the Islamic world and beyond. It would also send a signal to governments the world over that the rules of aggression have changed for them too, which could increase the risk of conflict between countries such as Russia and Georgia, India and Pakistan, and China and Taiwan.

Obviously, this debate is only just beginning on the Administration's new strategy for national security. But the debate is solidly grounded in American values and history. It will also be a debate among vast numbers of well-meaning Americans who have honest differences of opinion about the best way to use US military might. The debate will be contentious, but the stakes — in terms of both our national security and our allegiance to our core beliefs — are too high to ignore. I look forward to working closely with my colleagues in Congress to develop an effective and principled policy that will enable us to protect our national security and respect the basic principles that are essential for the world to be at peace.

24. JOHN F KENNEDY (1917–1963)

John Fitzgerald Kennedy was the thirty-fifth president of the US, from 1961 to 1963, and the youngest and the first Roman Catholic to be so elected.

The following is the inaugural address to the Congress on 20 January 1961, where he stresses 'Ask not what your country can do for you, but what you can do for your country.'

Vice President Johnson, Mr Speaker, Mr Chief Justice, President Eisenhower, Vice President Nixon, President Truman, reverend clergy, fellow citizens, we observe today not a victory of party, but a celebration of freedom — symbolising an end, as well as a beginning; signifying renewal, as well as change. For I have sworn before you and Almighty God the same solemn oath our forebears prescribed nearly a century and three quarters ago.

The world is very different now. For man holds in his mortal hands the power to abolish all forms of human poverty and all forms of human life. And yet the same revolutionary beliefs for which our forebears fought are still at issue around the globe — the belief that the rights of man come not from the generosity of the state, but from the hand of God.

We dare not forget today that we are the heirs of that first revolution. Let the word go forth from this time and place, to friend and foe alike, that the torch has been passed to a new generation of Americans — born in this century, tempered by war, disciplined by a hard and bitter peace, proud of our ancient heritage, and unwilling to witness or permit the slow undoing of those human rights to which this Nation has always been committed, and to which we are committed today at home and around the world.

Let every nation know, whether it wishes us well or ill, that we shall pay any price, bear any burden, meet any hardship, support any friend, oppose any foe, in order to assure the survival and the success of liberty.

This much we pledge—and more.

To those old allies whose cultural and spiritual origins we share, we pledge the loyalty of faithful friends. United, there is little we cannot do in a host of cooperative ventures. Divided, there is little we can do—for we dare not meet a powerful challenge at odds and split asunder.

To those new States whom we welcome to the ranks of the free, we pledge our word that one form of colonial control shall not have passed away merely to be replaced by a far more iron tyranny. We shall not always expect to find them supporting our view. But we shall always hope to find them strongly supporting their own freedom and to remember that, in the past, those who foolishly sought power by riding the back of the tiger ended up inside.

To those peoples in the huts and villages across the globe struggling to break the bonds of mass misery, we pledge our best efforts to help them help themselves, for whatever period is required—not because the Communists may be doing it, not because we seek their votes, but because it is right. If a free society cannot help the many who are poor, it cannot save the few who are rich.

To our sister republics south of our border, we offer a special pledge—to convert our good words into good deeds, in a new alliance for progress—to assist free men and free governments in casting off the chains of poverty. But this peaceful revolution of hope cannot become the prey of hostile powers. Let all our neighbours know that we shall join with them to oppose aggression or subversion anywhere in the Americas. And let every other power know that this Hemisphere intends to remain the master of its own house.

To that world assembly of sovereign states—the United Nations—our last best hope in an age where the instruments of war have far outpaced the instruments of peace, we renew our pledge of support: to prevent it from becoming merely a forum for invective, to strengthen its shield of the new and the weak, and to enlarge the area in which its writ may run.

Finally, to those nations who would make themselves our adversary, we offer not a pledge but a request: that both sides begin anew the quest for peace, before the dark powers of destruction unleashed by science engulf all humanity in planned or accidental self-destruction.

We dare not tempt them with weakness. For only when our arms are sufficient beyond doubt can we be certain beyond doubt that they will never be employed.

But neither can two great and powerful groups of nations take comfort from our present course—both sides overburdened by the cost of modern weapons, both rightly alarmed by the steady spread of the deadly atom, yet both racing to alter that uncertain balance of terror that stays the hand of mankind's final war.

So let us begin anew—remembering on both sides that civility is not a sign of weakness, and sincerity is always subject to proof. Let us never negotiate out of fear. But let us never fear to negotiate.

Let both sides explore what problems unite us instead of belabouring those problems which divide us.

Let both sides, for the first time, formulate serious and precise proposals for the inspection and control of arms and bring the absolute power to destroy other nations under the absolute control of all nations.

Let both sides seek to invoke the wonders of science instead of its terrors. Together let us explore the stars, conquer the deserts, eradicate disease, tap the ocean depths, and encourage the arts and commerce.

Let both sides unite to heed in all corners of the earth the command of Isaiah to undo the heavy burdens and to let the oppressed go free.

And if a beachhead of cooperation may push back the jungle of suspicion, let both sides join in creating a new endeavour, not a new balance of power, but a new world of law, where the strong are just and the weak secure and the peace preserved.

All this will not be finished in the first 100 days. Nor will it be finished in the first 1,000 days, nor in the life of this Administration, nor even perhaps in our lifetime on this planet. But let us begin.

In your hands, my fellow citizens, more than in mine, will rest the final success or failure of our course. Since this country was founded, each generation of Americans has been summoned to give testimony to its national loyalty. The graves of young Americans who answered the call to service surround the globe.

Now the trumpet summons us again—not as a call to bear arms, though arms we need; not as a call to battle, though embattled we are; but a call to bear the burden of a long twilight struggle, year in and year out, rejoicing in hope, patient in tribulation; a struggle against the common enemies of man: tyranny, poverty, disease, and war itself.

Can we forge against these enemies a grand and global alliance—North and South, East and West—that can assure a more fruitful life for all mankind? Will you join in that historic effort?

In the long history of the world, only a few generations have been granted the role of defending freedom in its hour of maximum danger. I do not shank from this responsibility. I welcome it. I do not believe that any of us would exchange places with any other people or any other generation. The energy, the faith, the devotion which we bring to this endeavour will light our country and all who serve it, and the glow from that fire can truly light the world.

And so, my fellow Americans: Ask not what your country can do for you, ask what you can do for your country.

My fellow citizens of the world: Ask not what America will do for you, but what together we can do for the freedom of man.

Finally, whether you are citizens of America or citizens of the world, ask of us the same high standards of strength and sacrifice which we ask of you. With a good conscience our only sure reward, with history the final judge of our deeds, let us go forth to lead the land we love, asking His blessing and His help, but knowing that here on earth God's work must truly be our own.

25. ROBERT F KENNEDY (1925–1968)

Robert Kennedy, the younger brother of John F Kennedy, was assasinated shortly after delivering a victory speech during the California Democratic Primaries.

On 4 April when Dr Martin Luther King was assassinated, Kennedy had broken the news to a large gathering of African Americans in Indianapolis, Indiana.

I have some very sad news for all of you, and, I think, sad news for all of our fellow citizens, and people who love peace all over the world, and that is that Martin Luther King was shot and was killed tonight in Memphis, Tennessee.

Martin Luther King dedicated his life to love and to justice between fellow human beings. He died in the cause of that effort. In this difficult day, in this difficult time for the United States, it's perhaps well to ask what kind of a nation we are and what direction we want to move in.

For those of you who are black—considering the evidence evidently is that there were white people who were responsible— you can be filled with bitterness, and with hatred, and a desire for revenge.

We can move in that direction as a country, in greater polarisation—black people amongst blacks, and white amongst whites, filled with hatred toward one another. Or we can make an effort, as Martin Luther King did, to understand and to comprehend, and replace that violence, that stain of bloodshed that has spread across our land, with an effort to understand, compassion and love.

For those of you who are black and are tempted to be filled with hatred and mistrust of the injustice of such an act, against all white people, I would only say that I can also feel in my own heart the same kind of feeling. I had a member of my family killed, but he was killed by a white man.

But we have to make an effort in the United States, we have to make an effort to understand, to get beyond these rather difficult times.

My favorite poet was Aeschylus. He once wrote: "Even in our sleep, pain which cannot forget falls drop by drop upon the heart, until, in our own despair, against our will, comes wisdom through the awful grace of God."

What we need in the United States is not division; what we need in the United States is not hatred; what we need in the United States is not violence and lawlessness, but is love and wisdom, and compassion toward one another, and a feeling of justice toward those who still suffer within our country, whether they be white or whether they be black.

So I ask you tonight to return home, to say a prayer for the family of Martin Luther King. Yeah that's true, but more importantly to say a prayer for our own country, which all of us love. A prayer for understanding and that compassion of which I spoke. We can do well in this country. We will have difficult times. We've had difficult times in the past. And we will have difficult times in the future. It is not the end of violence; it is not the end of lawlessness; and it's not the end of disorder.

But the vast majority of white people and the vast majority of black people in this country want to live together, want to improve the quality of our life, and want justice for all human beings that abide in our land.

Let us dedicate ourselves to what the Greeks wrote so many years ago: to tame the savageness of man and make gentle the life of this world. Let us dedicate ourselves to that, and say a prayer for our country and for our people.

Thank you very much.

26. REV. MARTIN LUTHER KING, JR.
(1929–1968)

Martin Luther King was an American clergyman, militant, non-violent civil rights leader and Negro integration leader.

The following is the 'I have a dream' speech delivered before the thousands assembled on the steps of the Lincoln Memorial, Washington, on 28 August 1963.

*F*ive score years ago, a great American, in whose symbolic shadow we stand today, signed the Emancipation Proclamation. This momentous decree came as a great beacon light of hope to millions of Negro slaves, who had been seared in the flames of withering injustice. It came as a joyous daybreak to end the long night of their captivity.

But one hundred years later, the Negro still is not free. One hundred years later, the life of the Negro is still sadly crippled by the manacles of segregation and the chains of discrimination. One hundred years later, the Negro lives on a lonely island of poverty in the midst of a vast ocean of material prosperity. One hundred years later, the Negro still languishes in the corners of American society and finds himself an exile in his own land.

So we've come here today to dramatise a shameful condition. In a sense, we've come to our nation's capital to cash a check. When the architects of our Republic wrote the magnificent words of the Constitution and the Declaration of Independence, they were signing a promissory note to which every American was to fall heir. This note was a promise that all men—yes, black men as well as white men—would be guaranteed the unalienable rights of life, liberty, and the pursuit of happiness.

It is obvious today that America has defaulted on this promissory note insofar as her citizens of colour are concerned.

Instead of honouring this sacred obligation, America has given the Negro people a bad cheque, a cheque which has come back marked "insufficient funds." But we refuse to believe that the bank of justice is bankrupt. We refuse to believe that there are insufficient funds in the great vaults of opportunity of this nation. So we've come to cash this cheque — a cheque that will give us upon demand the riches of freedom and the security of justice.

We have also come to this hallowed spot to remind America of the fierce urgency of *now*. This is no time to engage in the luxury of cooling off or to take the tranquillising drug of gradualism. Now is the time to make real the promises of democracy. Now is the time to rise from the dark and desolate valley of segregation to the sunlit path of racial justice. Now is the time to lift our nation from the quicksand of racial injustice to the solid rock of brotherhood. Now is the time to make justice a reality for all of God's children.

It would be fatal for the nation to overlook the urgency of the moment. This sweltering summer of the Negro's legitimate discontent will not pass until there is an invigorating autumn of freedom and equality. Nineteen sixth-three is not an end, but a beginning. Those who hope that the Negro needed to blow off steam and will now be content will have a rude awakening if the nation returns to business as usual. There will be neither rest nor tranquillity in America until the Negro is granted his citizenship rights. The whirlwinds of revolt will continue to shake the foundations of our nation until the bright day of justice emerges.

But that is something that I must say to my people who stand on the warm threshold which leads into the palace of justice. In the process of gaining our rightful place we must not be guilty of wrongful deeds. Let us not seek to satisfy our thirst for freedom by drinking from the cup of bitterness and hatred.

We must forever conduct our struggle on the high plane of dignity and discipline. We must not allow our creative protest to degenerate into physical violence. Again and again we must rise to the majestic heights of meeting physical force with soul force. The marvelous new militancy which has engulfed the Negro community must not lead us to a distrust of all white people, for many of our white brothers, as evidenced by their presence here today, have come to realise that their destiny is tied up with our destiny. And they have come to realise that their freedom is inextricably bound to our freedom. We cannot walk alone.

As we walk, we must make the pledge that we shall always march ahead. We cannot turn back. There are those who are asking the devotees of civil rights, "When will you be satisfied?" We can never be satisfied as long as the Negro is the victim of the unspeakable horrors of police brutality. We can never be satisfied as long as our bodies, heavy with the fatigue of travel, cannot gain lodging in the motels of the highways and the hotels of the cities. We cannot be satisfied as long as the Negro's basic mobility is from a smaller ghetto to a larger one. We can never be satisfied as long as our children are stripped of their selfhood and robbed of their dignity by signs stating "For Whites Only". We cannot be satisfied as long as a Negro in Mississippi cannot vote and a Negro in New York believes he has nothing for which to vote. No, no, we are not satisfied, and we will not be satisfied until justice rolls down like waters and righteousness like a mighty stream!

I am not unmindful that some of you have come here out of great trials and tribulations. Some of you have come fresh from narrow jail cells. Some of you have come from areas where your crest—quest for freedom left you battered by the storms of persecution and staggered by the winds of police brutality. You have been the veterans of creative suffering. Continue to work with the faith that unearned suffering is redemptive.

Go back to Mississippi, go back to Alabama, go back to South Carolina, go back to Georgia, go back to Louisiana, go back to the slums and ghettos of our Northern cities, knowing that somehow this situation can and will be changed. Let us not wallow in the valley of despair.

I say to you today, my friends, so even though we face the difficulties of today and tomorrow, I still have a dream. It is a dream deeply rooted in the American dream.

I have a dream that one day this nation will rise up and live out the true meaning of its creed: "We hold these truths to be self-evident that all men are created equal." I have a dream that one day on the red hills of Georgia, the sons of former slaves and the sons of former slaveowners will be able to sit down together at a table of brotherhood. I have a dream that one day, even the state of Mississippi, a desert state, sweltering with the heat of injustice and oppression, will be transformed into an oasis of freedom and justice. I have a dream that my four children will one day live in a nation where they will not be judged by the color of their skin but by the content of their character. I have a dream today.

I have a dream that one day the state of Alabama, whose governor's lips are presently dripping with the words of interposition and nullification, will be transformed into a situation where little black boys and black girls will be able to join hands with little white boys and white girls and walk together as sisters and brothers. I have a dream today. I have a dream that one day every valley shall be exalted, every hill and mountain shall be made low, the rough places will be made plain, and the crooked places will be made straight, and the glory of the Lord shall be revealed, and all flesh shall see it together. This is our hope. This is the faith with which I return to the South. With this faith we will be able to hew out of the mountain of despair a stone of hope. With this faith we will be able to transform the jangling discords of our nation into a beautiful symphony of brotherhood. With this faith we will be able to work together, to pray together, to struggle together, to go to jail together, to stand up for freedom together, knowing that we will be free one day.

This will be the day when all of God's children will be able to sing with a new meaning, "My country, 'tis of thee, sweet land of liberty, of thee I sing. Land where my fathers died, land of the pilgrim's pride, from every mountainside, let freedom ring." And if America is to be a great nation, this must become true. So let freedom ring from the prodigious hilltops of New Hampshire. Let freedom ring from the mighty mountains of New York. Let freedom ring from the heightening Alleghenies of Pennsylvania! Let freedom ring from the snowcapped Rockies of Colorado! Let freedom ring from the curvaceous peaks of California! But not only that; let freedom ring from Stone Mountain of Georgia! Let freedom ring from Lookout Mountain of Tennessee! Let freedom ring from every hill and every molehill of Mississippi. From every mountainside, let freedom ring.

When we let freedom ring, when we let it ring from every village and every hamlet, from every state and every city, we will be able to speed up that day when all of God's children — black men and white men, Jews and Gentiles, Protestants and

Catholics—will be able to join hands and sing in the words of the old Negro spiritual, "Free at last! free at last! thank God Almighty, we are free at last!"

27. VLADIMIR ILYICH LENIN (1870–1924)

Ilyich was a Russian revolutionary leader and statesman. He lead the revolution of 1917, liberating the country from the Tsars.

The following speech was delivered on 5 November 1921 to celebrate the anniversary of the October 1917 revolution.

The best way to celebrate the anniversary of a great revolution is to concentrate attention on its unsolved problems. It is particularly appropriate and necessary to celebrate the revision in this way at a time when we are faced with fundamental problems that the revolution has not yet solved, and when we must master something new — from the point of view of what the revolution has accomplished up to now — for the solution of these problems.

What is new for our revolution at the present time is the need for a reformist, gradual, cautious and roundabout approach to the solution of fundamental problems of economic development. This novelty gives rise to a number of questions, perplexities and doubts in both theory and practice.

A theoretical question. How can we explain the transition from a series of extremely revolutionary actions to extremely reformist actions in the same field at a time when the revolution as a whole is making victorious progress? Does it not imply a surrender of positions, an admission of defeat, or something of that sort? Of course, our enemies from the semi-feudal type of reactionaries to the Mensheviks or other knights of the Two-and-a-Half International, say that it does. They would not be enemies if they did not shout something of the sort on every pretext, and even without any pretext. The touching unanimity that prevails on this question among all parties, from the feudal reactionaries to the Mensheviks, is only further proof that all these parties constitute one reactionary mass opposed to the proletarian revolution—as Engels foresaw in his letters to Bebel of 1875 and 1884—be it said in parenthesis.

But there is perplexity, shall we say, among friends, too.

Restore large-scale industry, organise the direct exchange of its goods for the produce of small-peasant farming, and thus assist the socialisation of the latter. For the purpose of restoring large-scale industry, borrow from the peasants a certain quantity of foodstuffs and raw materials by requisitioning. This was the plan or method, system that we followed for more than three years, up to the spring of 1921. This was a revolutionary approach to the problem—to break up the old social-economic system completely at one stroke and to substitute a new one for it.

Since the spring of this approach, plan, method, or mode of action, we have been adopting—we have not yet adopted but are still adopting, and have not yet fully realised it—a totally different method, a reformist type of method: not to break up the old social-economic system—trade, petty production, petty proprietorship, capitalism—but to revive trade, petty proprietorship, capitalism, while cautiously and gradually getting the upper hand over them, or making it possible to subject them to state regulation only to the extent that they revive.

That is an entirely different approach to the problem.

Compared with the previous, revolutionary, approach, it is a reformist approach. Revolution is a change which breaks the old order to its very foundations, and not one that cautiously, slowly and gradually remodels it, taking care to break as little as possible.

The question that arises is this. If, after trying revolutionary methods, you find they have failed and adopt reformist methods, does it not prove that you are declaring the revolution to have been a mistake in general? Does it not prove that you should not have started with the revolution but should have started with reforms and confined yourselves to them?

That is the conclusion which the Mensheviks and other like them have drawn. But this conclusion is either sophistry, a mere fraud perpetrated by case-hardened politicians, or it is the childishness of political tyros. The greatest, perhaps, the only, danger to the genuine revolutionary is that of exaggerated revolutionism, ignoring the limits and conditions in which revolutionary methods are appropriate and can be successfully employed. True revolutionaries have mostly come a cropper when they began to write "revolution" with a capital R, to elevate revolution to something almost divine, to lose their heads, to lose the ability to reflect, weigh and ascertain the coolest and most dispassionate manner at what moment, under what circumstances and in which sphere of action you must act in a revolutionary manner, and at what moment, under what circumstances and in which sphere you must turn for reformist action. True revolutionaries will perish — not that they will be defeated from outside, but that their work will suffer internal collapse — only if they abandon their sober outlook and take it into their heads that the great, victorious, world revolution can and must solve all problems in a revolutionary manner under all circumstances and in all spheres of action. If they do this, their doom is certain.

Whoever gets such ideas into his head is lost because he has foolish ideas about a fundamental problem; and in a fierce war — and revolution is the fiercest sort of war — the penalty for folly is defeat.

What grounds are there for assuming that the great, victorious, world revolution can and must employ only revolutionary methods? There are none at all. The assumption is a pure fallacy. This can be proved by purely theoretical propositions if we stick to Marxism. The experience of our revolution also shows that it is a fallacy. From the theoretical point of view, foolish things are done at the time of revolution just as at any other time, said Engels, and he was right. We must try to do as few foolish things as possible, and rectify those that are done as quickly as possible, and we must, as soberly as we can, estimate which problems can be solved by revolutionary methods at any given time and which cannot. From the point the view of our practical experience, the Brest peace was an example of action that was not revolutionary at all. It was reformist and even worse, because it was a retreat; whereas, as a general rule, reformist action advances slowly, cautiously, gradually, and does not move backward. The proof that our tactics in concluding the Brest peace were correct is now so complete, so obvious to all and generally admitted, that there is no need to say anymore about it.

Our revolution has completed only its bourgeois-democratic work; and we have every right to be proud of this. The proletarian or socialist part of its work may be summed up in three main points: (1) The revolutionary withdrawal from the imperialist world war; the exposure and halting of the slaughter organised by the two world groups of capitalist predators. For our part we have done this in full. Others could have done it only if there had been a revolution in a number of advanced countries. (2) The establishment of the Soviet system, as a form of the dictatorship of the proletariat. An epoch-making change has been made. The era of bourgeois-democratic parliamentarism has come to an end. A new chapter in world history — the era of proletarian dictatorship — has been opened. The Soviet system and all forms of proletarian dictatorship will have the finishing touches put to them and be completed only by the efforts of a number of countries. There is still a great deal we have not done in this field. It would be unpardonable to lose sight of this. Again and again we shall have to improve the work, redo it, start from the beginning. Every step onward and upward that we take in developing our productive forces and our culture must be accompanied by the work of improving and altering our Soviet system. We are still low in the scale of economics and culture. Much will have to be altered, and to be embarrassed by this would be absurd, if not worse. (3) The creation of the economic basis of the socialist system; the main features of what is most important, most fundamental, have not yet been completed. This, however, is our soundest basis, soundest from the point of view of principle and from the practical point of view, from the point of view of the RSFSR today and from the international point of view.

Since the main features of this basis have not yet been completed, we must concentrate all our attention upon it. The difficulty here lies in the form of the transition.

In April 1918, in my *Immediate Tasks of the Soviet Government,* I wrote:

"It is not enough to be a revolutionary and an adherent of socialism or a Communist in general. You must be able at each particular moment to find the particular link in the chain which you must grasp with all your might in order to hold the whole chain and to prepare firmly for the transition to the next link; the order of the links, their form, the manner in which they are linked together, their difference from each other in the historical chain of events are not as simple and not as senseless as those in an ordinary chain made by a smith."

At the present time, in the sphere of activity with which we are dealing, this link is the revival of home trade under proper state regulation—direction. Trade is the link in the historical chain of events, in the transitional forms of our socialist construction in 1921-22, which we, the proletarian government, we, the ruling Communist Party must grasp with all our might. If we grasp this link firmly enough now we shall certainly control the whole chain in the very near future. If we do not, we shall not control the whole chain, we shall not create the foundation for socialist social and economic relations.

Communism and trade? It sounds strange. The two seem to be unconnected, incongruous, poles apart. But if we study it from the point of view of economics, we shall find that one is no more remote from the other than communism is from small-peasant, patriarchal farming.

When we are victorious on a world scale, I think we shall use gold for the purpose of building public lavatories in the streets of some of the largest cities of the world. This would be the most just and most educational way of utilising gold for the benefit of those generations which have not forgotten how, for the sake of gold, ten million men were killed and thirty million maimed in the great war for freedom, the war of 1914-18, the war that was waged to decide the great question of which peace was the worst, that of Brest or that of Versailles; and how, for the sake of this same gold, they certainly intend to kill twenty million men and to maim sixty million in a war, say, in 1925, or 1928, between, say, Japan and the USA, or between Britain and the USA, or something like that.

But however just, useful, or humane it would be to utilise gold for this purpose, we nevertheless say that we must work for another decade or two with the same intensity and with the same success as in the 1917-21 period, only in a much wider field, in order to reach this stage. Meanwhile, we must save the gold in the RSFSR, sell it at the highest price, buy goods with it at the lowest price. When you live among wolves, you must howl like a wolf, while as for exterminating all the wolves, as should be done in a rational human society; we shall act up to the wise Russian proverb: Boast not before but after the battle.

Trade is the only possible economic link between the scores of millions of small farmers and large-scale machine industry with a network of power transmission lines, an industry whose technical equipment, organisational superstructures and other features are sufficient to enable it to supply the small farmers with the best goods in larger quantities, more quickly and more cheaply than before. On a world scale this *if* has already been achieved, this condition already exists. But the country, which tried alone directly and at one stroke to create, to put into use, to organise practically the new links between industry and agriculture, failed to achieve this task by direct assault, and must now try to achieve it by a number of slow, gradual, and cautious siege operations.

The proletarian government can control trade, direct it into definite channels, keep it within certain limits. I shall give a small, a very small example. In the Donets Basin, a slight, still very slight, but undoubted revival in the economy has commenced, partly due to a rise in the productivity of labour at the large state mines, and partly due to the leasing of small mines to peasants. As a result, the proletarian government is receiving a small additional quantity—a miserably small quantity compared with what is obtained in the advanced countries, but an appreciable quantity, considering our poverty-stricken condition—of coal at a cost of, say, 100; and it is selling this coal too various government departments at a price of, say, 120, and to private individuals at a price of, say, 140. I must say in parenthesis that my figures are quite arbitrary, first, because I do not know the exact figures, and secondly, I would not now make them public even if I did. This looks as if we are beginning, if only in very modest dimensions, to control exchange between industry and agriculture, to control wholesale trade, to cope with the task of taking in hand the available small, backward industry, of large-scale but weakened and ruined industry; of reviving trade on the present economic basis; of making the ordinary middle peasant—and that is the typical peasant, the peasant-in-the-mass, the true representative of the petty-bourgeois milieu—feel the benefit of the economic revival; of taking advantage of it for the purpose of more systematically and persistently, more widely and successfully restoring large-scale industry.

We shall not surrender to 'sentimental socialism', or to the old Russian, semi-aristocratic, semi-muzhik and patriarchal mood, with their supreme contempt for trade. We can use, and since it is necessary, we must learn to use, all transitional economic forms for the purpose of immediately reviving the economy of our ruined and tormented country, of improving industry, and facilitating such future, more extensive and more deep-going measures as electrification.

Marxism alone has precisely and correctly defined the relation of reforms to revolution, although Marx was able to see this relation only from one aspect — under the conditions preceding the first to any extent permanent and lasting victory of the proletariat, if only in one country. Under those conditions, the basis of the proper relation was that reforms are a by-product of the revolutionary class struggle of the foundation of the revolutionary tactics of the proletariat — the ABC, which is being distorted and obscured by the corrupt leaders of the Second International and the half-pedantic and half-finicky knights of the Two-and-a-Half International. After the victory of the proletariat, if only in one country, something new enters into the relation between reforms and revolution. In principle, it is same as before, but a change in form takes place, which Marx himself could not foresee, but which can be appreciated only on the basis of the philosophy and politics of Marxism. Why were we able to carry out the Breast retreat successfully? Because we had advanced so far that we had room in which to retreat. At such dizzy speed, in a few weeks, from October 25, 1917, to the Brest peace, we built up the Soviet state, withdrew from the imperialist war in a revolutionary manner and completed the bourgeois-democratic revolution so that even the great backward movement — the Brest peace — left us sufficient room in which to take advantage of the respite and to march forward victoriously against Kolchak, Denikin, Yudenich, Pilsudski and Wrangel.

Before the victory of the proletariat, reforms are a by-product of the revolutionary class struggle. After the victory — while still remaining a by-product on an international scale — they are, in addition, for the country in which victory has been achieved, a necessary and legitimate breathing space when, after the utmost exertion of effort, it becomes obvious that sufficient strength is lacking for the revolutionary accomplishment of some transition or another. Victory creates such a reserve of strength that it is possible to hold out even in a forced retreat, hold out both materially and morally. Holding out materially means preserving a sufficient superiority of forces to prevent the enemy from inflicting utter defeat. Holding out morally means not allowing oneself to become demoralised and disorganised, keeping a sober view of the situation, preserving vigour and firmness of spirit, even retreating a long way, but not too far, and in such a way as to stop the retreat in time and revert to the offensive.

We retreated to state capitalism, but we did not retreat too far. We are now retreating to the state regulation of trade, but we shall not retreat too far. There are visible signs that the retreat is coming to an end; there are signs that we shall be able to stop this retreat in the not too distant future. The more conscious, the more unanimous, the more free from prejudice we are in carrying out this necessary retreat, the sooner shall we be able to stop it, and the more lasting, speedy and extensive will be our subsequent victorious advance.

28. ABRAHAM LINCOLN (1809–1865)

Lincoln was the sixteenth president of the US, elected in 1861.
His famous Gettysburg speech on 19 November 1863, with its
ending words – government of the people, by the people, for the people –
have come to symbolise the definition of democracy itself.

*F*our score and seven years ago our fathers brought forth on this continent, a new nation, conceived in liberty, and dedicated to the proposition that all men are created equal.

Now we are engaged in a great civil war, testing whether that nation, or any nation so conceived and so dedicated, can long endure. We are met on a great battlefield of that war. We have come to dedicate a portion of that field, as a final resting place for those who here gave their lives that that nation might live. It is altogether fitting and proper that we should do this.

But in a larger sense, we cannot dedicate, we cannot consecrate, we cannot hallow, this ground. The brave men, living and dead, who struggled here, have consecrated it, far above our poor power to add or detract. The world will little note, nor long remember, what we say here, but it can never forget what they did here. It is for us the living, rather, to be dedicated here to the unfinished work which they who fought here have thus far so nobly advanced. It is rather for us to be here dedicated to the great task remaining before us – that from these honoured dead we take increased devotion to that cause for which they gave the last full measure of devotion; that we here highly resolve that these dead shall not have died in vain; that this nation, under God, shall have a new birth of freedom; and that government of the people, by the people, for the people, shall not perish from the earth.

29. NELSON MANDELA (1918–)

Nelson Rohihlala Mandela was the first black president of South Africa, elected in 1994. A renowned lawyer and politician, he led the South Africans to a non-racist democracy.

He was imprisoned for 27 years, from 1960. The following speech was given on 21 September 1953, well before his imprisonment.

Since 1912 and year after year thereafter, in their homes and local areas, in provincial and national gatherings, on trains and buses, in the factories and on the farms, in cities, villages, shanty towns, schools and prisons, the African people have discussed the shameful misdeeds of those who rule the country. Year after year, they have raised their voices in condemnation of the grinding poverty of the people, the low wages, the acute shortage of land, the inhuman exploitation and the whole policy of white domination. But instead of more freedom, repression began to grow in volume and intensity, and it seemed that all their sacrifices would end up in smoke and dust. Today the entire country knows that their labours were not in vain for a new spirit, and new ideas have gripped our people. Today the people speak the language of action. There is a mighty awakening among the men and women of our country and the year 1952 stands out as the year of this upsurge of national consciousness.

In June, 1952, the African National Congress and the South African Indian Congress, bearing in mind their responsibility as the representatives of the downtrodden and oppressed people of South Africa, took the plunge and launched the Campaign for the Defiance of the Unjust Laws. Starting off in Port Elizabeth in the early hours of June 26 and with only thirty-three defiers in action and then in Johannesburg in the afternoon of the same day with one hundred and six defiers, it spread throughout the country like wild fire. Factory and office workers, doctors, lawyers, teachers, students and the clergy; Africans, Coloureds, Indians and Europeans, old and young, all rallied to the national call and defied the pass laws and the curfew and the railway apartheid regulations. At the end of the year, more than 8,000 people of all races had defied. The campaign called for immediate and heavy sacrifices. Workers lost their jobs, chiefs and teachers were expelled from the service, doctors, lawyers and businessmen gave up their practices and businesses and elected to go to jail. Defiance was a step of great political significance. It released strong social forces which affected thousands of our countrymen. It was an effective way of getting the masses to function politically; a powerful method of voicing our indignation against the reactionary policies of the Government. It was one of the best ways of exerting pressure on the Government and extremely dangerous to the stability and security of the state. It inspired and aroused our people from a conquered and servile community of yes-men to a militant and uncompromising band of comrades-in-arms. The entire country was transformed into battle zones where the forces of liberation were locked up in immortal conflict against those of reaction and evil. Our flag flew in every battlefield and thousands of our countrymen rallied around it. We held the initiative and the forces of freedom were advancing on all fronts. It was against this background and at the height of this campaign that we held our last annual provincial conference in Pretoria from the 10th to the 12th of October last year. In a way, that conference was a welcome reception for those who had returned from the battlefields and a farewell to those who were still going to action. The spirit of defiance and action dominated the entire conference.

Today we meet under totally different conditions. By the end of July last year, the campaign had reached a stage where it had to be suppressed by the Government or it would impose its own policies on the country.

The government launched its reactionary offensive and struck at us. Between July last year and August this year, forty-seven leading members from both Congresses in Johannesburg, Port Elizabeth and Kimberley were arrested, tried and convicted for launching the Defiance Campaign and given suspended sentences ranging from three months to two years on condition that they did not again participate in the defiance of the unjust laws. In

November last year, a proclamation was passed which prohibited meetings of more than ten Africans and made it an offence for any person to call upon an African to defy. Contravention of this proclamation carried a penalty of three years or of a fine of three hundred pounds. In March this year, the Government passed the so-called Public Safety Act which empowered it to declare a state of emergency and to create conditions which would permit of the most ruthless and pitiless methods of suppressing our movement. Almost simultaneously, the Criminal Laws Amendment Act was passed which provided heavy penalties for those convicted of defiance offences. This Act also made provision for the whipping of defiers including women. It was under this Act that Mr Arthur Matlala who was the local [leader] of the Central Branch during the Defiance Campaign, was convicted and sentenced to twelve months with hard labour plus eight strokes by the magistrate of Villa Nora. The Government also made extensive use of the Suppression of Communism Act.

You will remember that in May last year the Government ordered Moses Kotane, Yusuf Dadoo, J B Marks, David Bopape and Johnson Ngwevela to resign from the Congresses and many other organisations and were also prohibited from attending political gatherings. In consequence of these bans, Moses Kotane, J B Marks, and David Bopape did not attend our last provincial conference. In December last year, the Secretary General, Mr W M Sisulu, and I were banned from attending gatherings and confined to Johannesburg for six months. Early this year, the President-General, Chief Luthuli, whilst in the midst of a national tour which he was prosecuting with remarkable energy and devotion, was prohibited for a period of twelve months from attending public gatherings and from visiting Durban, Johannesburg, Cape Town, Port Elizabeth and many other centres. A few days before the president-general was banned, the president of the SAIC, Dr G M Naicker, had been served with a similar notice. Many other active workers both from the African and Indian Congresses and from trade union organisations were also banned.

The Congresses realised that these measures created a new situation which did not prevail when the campaign was launched in June 1952. The tide of defiance was bound to recede and we were forced to pause and to take stock of the new situation. We had to analyse the dangers that faced us, formulate plans to overcome them and evolve new plans of political struggle. A political movement must keep in touch with reality and the prevailing conditions. Long speeches, the shaking of fists, the banging of tables and strongly-worded resolutions out of touch with the objective conditions do not bring about mass action and can do a great deal of harm to the organisation and the struggle we serve. The masses had to be prepared and made ready for new forms of political struggle. We had to recuperate our strength and muster our forces for another and more powerful offensive against the enemy. To have gone ahead blindly as if nothing had happened would have been suicidal and stupid. The conditions under which we meet today are, therefore, vastly different. The Defiance Campaign, together with its thrills and adventures, has receded. The old methods of bringing about mass action through public mass meetings, press statements and leaflets calling upon the people to go to action have become extremely dangerous and difficult to use effectively. The authorities will not easily permit a meeting called under the auspices of the ANC, few newspapers will publish statements openly criticising the policies of the Government and there is hardly a single printing press which will agree to print leaflets calling upon workers to embark on industrial action for fear of prosecution under the Suppression of Communism Act and similar measures. These developments require the evolution of new forms of political struggle which will make it reasonable for us to strive for action on a higher level than the Defiance Campaign. The Government, alarmed at the indomitable upsurge of national consciousness, is doing everything in its power to crush our movement by removing the genuine representatives of the people from the organisations. According to a statement made by Swart in Parliament on the 18th September, 1953, there are thirty-three trade union officials and eighty-nine other people who have been served with notices in terms of the Suppression of Communism Act. This does not include that formidable array of freedom fighters who have been named and blacklisted under the Suppression of Communism Act and those who have been banned under the Riotous Assemblies Act.

Meanwhile the living conditions of the people, already extremely difficult, are steadily worsening and becoming unbearable. The purchasing power of the masses is progressively declining and the cost of living is rocketing. Bread is now dearer than it was two months ago. The cost of milk, meat and vegetables is beyond the pockets of the average family and many of our people cannot afford them. The people are too poor to have enough food to feed their families and children. They cannot afford sufficient clothing, housing and medical care. They are denied the right to security in the event of unemployment, sickness, disability, old age and where these exist, they are of an extremely inferior and useless nature. Because of lack of proper medical amenities our people are ravaged by such dreaded diseases as tuberculosis, venereal disease, leprosy, pellagra, and infantile mortality is very high. The recent state budget made provision for the increase of the cost-of-living allowances for Europeans and not a word was said about the poorest and most hard-hit section of the population— the African people.

The insane policies of the Government which have brought about an explosive situation in the country have definitely scared away foreign capital from South Africa and the financial crisis through which the country is now passing is forcing many industrial and business concerns to close down, to retrench their staffs and unemployment is growing every day. The farm labourers are in a particularly dire plight. You will perhaps recall the investigations and exposures of the semi-slave conditions on the Bethal farms made in 1948 by the Reverend Michael Scott and a Guardian correspondent; by the Drum last year and the Advance in April this year.

You will recall how human beings, wearing only sacks with holes for their heads and arms, never given enough food to eat, slept on cement floors on cold nights with only their sacks to cover their shivering bodies. You will remember how they are woken up as early as 4 a.m. and taken to work on the fields with the indunas sjambokking those who tried to straighten their backs, who felt weak and dropped down because of hunger and sheer exhaustion. You will also recall the story of human beings toiling pathetically from the early hours of the morning till sunset, fed only on mealie meal served on filthy sacks spread on the ground and eating with their dirty hands. People falling ill and never once being given medical attention. You will also recall the revolting story of a farmer who was convicted for tying a labourer by his feet from a tree and had him flogged to death, pouring boiling water into his mouth whenever he cried for water. These things which have long vanished from many parts of the world still flourish in SA today. None will deny that they constitute a serious challenge to Congress and we are in duty bound to find an effective remedy for these obnoxious practices.

The Government has introduced in Parliament the Native Labour (Settlement of Disputes) Bill and the Bantu Education Bill. Speaking on the Labour Bill, the Minister of Labour, Ben Schoeman, openly stated that the aim of this wicked measure is to bleed African trade unions to death. By forbidding strikes and lockouts, it deprives Africans of the one weapon the workers have to improve their position. The aim of the measure is to destroy the present African trade unions which are controlled by the workers themselves and which fight for the improvement of their working conditions in return for a Central Native Labour Board controlled by the Government and which will be used to frustrate the legitimate aspirations of the African worker. The Minister of Native Affairs, Verwoerd, has also been brutally clear in explaining the objects of the Bantu Education Bill. According to him, the aim of this law is to teach our children that Africans are inferior to Europeans. African education would be taken out of the hands of people who taught equality between black and white. When this Bill becomes law, it will not be the parents but the Department of Native Affairs which will decide whether an African child should receive higher or other education. It might well be that the children of those who criticise the Government and who fight its policies will almost certainly be taught how to drill rocks in the mines and how to plough potatoes on the farms of Bethal. High education might well be the privilege of those children whose families have a tradition of collaboration with the ruling circles.

The attitude of the Congress on these bills is very clear and unequivocal. Congress totally rejects both bills without reservation. The last provincial Conference strongly condemned the then proposed Labour Bill as a measure designed to rob the African workers of the universal right of free trade unionism and to undermine and destroy the existing African trade unions. The conference further called upon the African workers to boycott and defy the application of this sinister scheme which was calculated to further the exploitation of the African worker. To accept a measure of this nature even in a qualified manner would be a betrayal of the toiling masses. At a time when every genuine Congressite should fight unreservedly for the recognition of African trade unions and the realisation of the principle that everyone has the right to form and to join trade unions for the protection of his interests, we declare our firm belief in the principles enunciated in the Universal Declaration of Human Rights that everyone has the right to education; that education shall be directed to the full development of human personality and to the strengthening of respect for human rights and fundamental freedoms. It shall promote understanding, tolerance and friendship among the nations, racial or religious groups and shall further the activities of the United Nations for the maintenance of peace. That parents have the right to choose the kind of education that shall be given to their children.

The cumulative effect of all these measures is to prop up and perpetuate the artificial and decaying policy of the supremacy of the white men. The attitude of the government to us is that "Let's beat them down with guns and batons and trample them under our feet. We must be ready to drown the whole country in blood if only there is the slightest chance of preserving white supremacy."

But there is nothing inherently superior about the herrenvolk idea of the supremacy of the whites. In China, India, Indonesia and Korea, American, British, Dutch and French Imperialism, based on the concept of the supremacy of Europeans over Asians, has been completely and perfectly exploded. In Malaya and Indo-China, British and French imperialisms are being shaken to their foundations by powerful and revolutionary national liberation movements. In Africa, there are approximately 190,000,000 Africans as against 4,000,000 Europeans. The entire continent is seething with discontent and already there are powerful revolutionary eruptions in the Gold Coast, Nigeria, Tunisia, Kenya, the Rhodesias and South Africa. The oppressed people and the oppressors are at loggerheads. The day of reckoning between the forces of freedom and those of reaction is not very far off. I have not the slightest doubt that when that day comes truth and justice will prevail.

The intensification of repressions and the extensive use of the bans is designed to immobilise every active worker and to check the national liberation movement. But gone forever are the days when harsh and wicked laws provided the oppressors with years of peace and quiet. The racial policies of the Government have pricked the conscience of all men of good will and have aroused their deepest indignation. The feelings of the oppressed people have never been more bitter. If the ruling circles seek to maintain their position by such inhuman methods then a clash between the forces of freedom and those of reaction is certain. The grave plight of the people compels them to resist to the death the stinking policies of the gangsters that rule our country.

But in spite of all the difficulties outlined above, we have won important victories. The general political level of the people has been considerably raised and they are now more conscious of their strength. Action has become the language of the day. The ties between the working people and the Congress have been greatly strengthened. This is a development of the highest importance because in a country such as ours a political organisation that does not receive the support of the workers is in fact paralysed on the very ground on which it has chosen to wage battle. Leaders of trade union organisations are at the same time important officials of the provincial and local branches of the ANC. In the past, we talked of the African, Indian and Coloured struggles. Though certain individuals raised the question of a united front of all the oppressed groups, the various non-European organisations stood miles apart from one another and the efforts of those for coordination and unity were like a voice crying in the wilderness and it seemed that the day would never dawn when the oppressed people would stand and fight together shoulder to shoulder against a common enemy. Today we talk of the struggle of the oppressed people which, though it is waged through their respective autonomous organisations, is gravitating towards one central command.

Our immediate task is to consolidate these victories, to preserve our organisations and to muster our forces for the resumption of the offensive. To achieve this important task, the National Executive of the ANC, in consultation with the National Action Committee of the ANC and the SAIC, formulated a plan of action popularly known as the "M Plan" and the highest importance is [given] to it by the National Executives. Instructions were given to all provinces to implement the M Plan without delay.

The underlying principle of this plan is the understanding that it is no longer possible to wage our struggle mainly on the old methods of public meetings and printed circulars. The aim is

to consolidate the Congress machinery;

to enable the transmission of important decisions taken on a national level to every member of the organisation without calling public meetings, issuing press statements and printing circulars;

to build up in the local branches themselves local Congresses which will effectively represent the strength and will of the people;

to extend and strengthen the ties between Congress and the people and to consolidate Congress leadership.

This plan is being implemented in many branches not only in the Transvaal but also in the other provinces and is producing excellent results. The Regional Conferences held in Sophiatown, Germiston, Kliptown and Benoni on the 28th June, 23rd and 30th August and on the 6th September, 1953, which were attended by large crowds, are a striking demonstration of the effectiveness of this plan, and the national executives must be complimented for it. I appeal to all members of the Congress to redouble their efforts and play their part truly and well in its implementation. The hard, dirty and strenuous task of recruiting members and strengthening our organisation through a house-to-house campaign in every locality must be done by you all. From now on the activity of Congressites must not be confined to speeches and resolutions. Their activities must find expression in wide scale work among the masses, work which will enable them to make the greatest possible contact with the working people. You must protect and defend your trade unions. If you are not allowed to have your meetings publicly, then you must hold them over your machines in the factories, on the trains and buses as you travel home. You must have them in your villages and shanty towns. You must make every home, every shack and every mud structure where our people live, a branch of the trade union movement and never surrender.

You must defend the right of African parents to decide the kind of education that shall be given to their children. Teach the children that Africans are not one iota inferior to Europeans. Establish your own community schools where the right kind of education will be given to our children. If it becomes dangerous or impossible to have these alternative schools, then again you must make every home, every shack or rickety structure a centre of learning for our children. Never surrender to the inhuman and barbaric theories of Verwoerd.

The decision to defy the unjust laws enabled Congress to develop considerably wider contacts between itself and the masses and the urge to join Congress grew day by day. But due to the fact that the local branches did not exercise proper control and supervision, the admission of new members was not carried out satisfactorily. No careful examination was made of their past history and political characteristics. As a result of this, there were many shady characters ranging from political clowns, place-seekers, splitters, saboteurs, agents-provocateurs to informers and even policemen, who infiltrated into the ranks of Congress. One need only refer to the Johannesburg trial of Dr. Moroka and nineteen others, where a member of Congress who actually worked at the National Headquarters, turned out to be a detective-sergeant on special duty. Remember the case of Leballo of Brakpan who wormed himself into that branch by producing faked naming letters from the Liquidator, De Villiers Louw, who had instructions to spy on us. There are many other similar instances that emerged during the Johannesburg, Port Elizabeth and Kimberley trials.

Whilst some of these men were discovered, there are many who have not been found out. In Congress, there are still many shady characters, political clowns, place-seekers, saboteurs, provocateurs, informers and policemen who masquerade as progressives but who are in fact the bitterest enemies of our organisation. Outside appearances are highly deceptive and we cannot classify these men by looking at their faces or by listening to their sweet tongues or their vehement speeches demanding immediate action. The friends of the people are distinguishable by the ready and disciplined manner in which they rally behind their organisation and their readiness to sacrifice when the preservation of the organisation has become a matter of life and death. Similarly, enemies and shady characters are detected by the extent to which they consistently attempt to wreck the organisation by creating fratricidal strife, disseminating confusion and undermining and even opposing important plans of action to vitalise the organisation. In this respect it is interesting to note that almost all the people who oppose the M Plan are people who have consistently refused to respond when sacrifices were called for, and whose political background leaves much to be desired. These shady characters by means of flattery, bribes and corruption, win the support of the weak-willed and politically backward individuals, detach them from Congress and use them in their own interests. The presence of such elements in Congress constitutes a serious threat to the struggle, for the capacity for political action of an organisation which is ravaged by such disruptive and splitting elements is considerably undermined. Here in South Africa, as in many parts of the world, a revolution is maturing: it is the profound desire, the determination and the urge of the overwhelming majority of the country to destroy for ever the shackles of oppression that condemn them to servitude and slavery. To overthrow oppression has been sanctioned by humanity and is the highest aspiration of every free man. If elements in our organisation seek to impede the realisation of this lofty purpose then these people have placed themselves outside the organisation and must be put out of action before they do more harm. To do otherwise would be a crime and a serious neglect of duty. We must rid ourselves of such elements and give our organisation the striking power of a real militant mass organisation.

Kotane, Marks, Bopape, Tloome and I have been banned from attending gatherings and we cannot join and counsel with you on the serious problems that are facing our country. We have been banned because we champion the freedom of the oppressed people of our country and because we have consistently fought against the policy of racial discrimination in favour of a policy which accords fundamental human rights to all, irrespective of race, colour, sex or language. We are exiled from our own people, for we have uncompromisingly resisted the efforts of imperialist America and her satellites to drag the world into the rule of violence and brutal force, into the rule of the napalm, hydrogen and the cobalt bombs where millions of people will be wiped out to satisfy the criminal and greedy appetites of the imperial powers. We have been gagged because we have emphatically and openly condemned the criminal attacks by the imperialists against the people of Malaya, Vietnam, Indonesia, Tunisia and Tanganyika and called upon our people to identify themselves unreservedly with the cause of world peace and to fight against the war policies of America and her satellites. We are being shadowed, hounded and trailed because we fearlessly voiced our horror and indignation at the slaughter of the people of Korea and Kenya. The massacre of the Kenya people by Britain has aroused worldwide indignation and protest. Children are being burnt alive, women are raped, tortured, whipped and boiling water poured on their breasts to force confessions from them that Jomo Kenyatta had administered the Mau Mau oath to them. Men are being castrated and shot dead. In the Kikuyu country, there are some villages in which the population has been completely wiped out. We are prisoners in our own country because we dared to raise our voices against these horrible atrocities and because we expressed our solidarity with the cause of the Kenya people.

You can see that there is no easy walk to freedom anywhere, and many of us will have to pass through the valley of the shadow — of death — again and again before we reach the mountain tops of our desires.

Dangers and difficulties have not deterred us in the past, they will not frighten us now. But we must be prepared for them like men in business who do not waste energy in vain talk and idle action. The way of preparation — for action — lies in our rooting out all impurity and indiscipline from our organisation and making it the bright and shining instrument that will cleave its way to freedom.

30. KARL MARX (1818–1883)

Karl Marx was a great German socialist thinker and the founder of communalism.

While in exile in England, he delivered this speech at the founding of the People's Party in London in 1856.

The revolutions of 1848 were but poor incidents – small fractures and fissures in the dry crust of European society. However, they announced the abyss. Beneath the apparently solid surface, they betrayed oceans of liquid matter, only needing expansion to rend into fragments continents of hard rock. Noisily and confusedly they proclaimed the emancipation of the proletariat, that is, the secret of the nineteenth century, and of the revolutions. It is true: there was no novelty invented in 1848. Steam, electricity, and the self-acting mule were revolutionists of a rather more dangerous character than even citizens – Barbes, Raspail, and Blanqui. But, although the atmosphere in which we live weighs upon everyone with a twenty thousand pound force, do you feel it? No more than European society before 1848 felt the revolutionary atmosphere enveloping and pressing it from all sides. There is one great fact, characteristic of this, our nineteenth century – a fact which no party dares deny. On the other hand, there exist symptoms of decay far surpassing the horrors recorded in the later times of the Roman Empire. In our days, everything seems pregnant to the contrary; machinery gifted with the wonderful power of shortening and fructifying human labour, we behold starving and overworking it. The new-fangled sources of wealth, by some strange, weird spell, are turned into sources of want. The victories of art seem bought by the loss of character. At the same pace that mankind masters nature, man seems to become enslaved to other men or to his own infamy. Even the pure light of science seems unable to shine but on the dark background of ignorance. All our inventions and progress seem to result in endowing material forces with intellectual life, and in satisfying human life into a material force.

This antagonism between modern industry and science on the one hand, modern misery and dissolution on the other; this antagonism between the productive powers and the social relations of our epoch is a fact, palpable, overwhelming, and not to be controverted. Some parties may wail over it; others may wish to get rid of modern arts in order to get rid of modern conflicts. Or they may imagine so signal a regress in politics. On our part, we do not mistake the shape of the shrewd spirit that continues to mark all these contradictions. We know that to work well the new-fangled forces of society, they only want to be mastered by new-fangled men—and such are the working men. They are as much the invention of modern time as machinery itself. In the signs that bewilder the middle class, the aristocracy, and the poor prophets of regression, we do recognise our brave friend, Robin Goodfellow, the old more, that can work on the earth so fast, the worthy pioneer—the revolution. The English working men are the firstborn sons of modern industry. They will then, certainly, not be the last in aiding the social revolution produced by that industry, a revolution which means the emancipation of their own class all over the world, which is universal as capital-rule and wages-slavery. I know the heroic struggles the English working class have gone through since the middle of the last century—struggles less glorious because they are shrouded in obscurity and buried by the middle-class historians to revenge the misdeeds of the ruling class. There existed in the Middle Ages in Germany a secret tribunal called the Vehmgericht. If a red cross was seen marked on a house, people knew its owner was doomed by the Vehm. All the houses of Europe are now marked with a mysterious red cross. History is the judge—its executioner, the proletarian.

31. JAMES MONROE (1758–1831)

James Monroe was the president of the US from 1817 to 1825. His doctrine, that the American continent should not be colonised by a European power, became famous.
He gave this speech on 2 December 1823 in Washington.

*F*ellow-Citizens of the Senate and House of Representatives: Many important subjects will claim your attention during the present session, of which I shall endeavour to give, in aid of your deliberations, a just idea in this communication. I undertake this duty with diffidence, from the vast extent of the interests on which I have to treat and of their great importance to every portion of our Union. I enter on it with zeal from a thorough conviction that there never was a period since the establishment of our revolution when, regarding the condition of the civilised world and its bearing upon us, there was greater necessity for devotion in public servants to their respective duties, or for virtue, patriotism, and union in our constituents.

At the proposal of the Russian imperial government, made through the minister of the emperor residing here, a full power and instructions have been transmitted to the minister of the United States at St Petersburg to arrange by amicable negotiation the respective rights and interests of the two nations on the northwest coast of this continent. A similar proposal has been made by his Imperial Majesty to the government of Great Britain, which has likewise been acceded to. The government of the United States has been desirous by this friendly proceeding of manifesting the great value which they have inevitably attached to the friendship of the emperor and their solicitude to cultivate the best understanding with his government. In the discussions to which this interest has given rise and in the arrangements by which they may terminate, the occasion has been judged proper for asserting, as a principle in which the rights and interests of the United States are involved, that the American continents, by the free and independent condition which they have assumed and maintain, are henceforth not to be considered as subjects for future colonization by any European powers.

It was stated at the commencement of the last session that a great effort was then making in Spain and Portugal to improve the condition of the people of those countries, and that it appeared to be conducted with extraordinary moderation. It need scarcely be remarked that the result has been so far very different from what was then anticipated. Of events in that quarter of the globe, with which we have so much intercourse and from which we derive our origin, we have always been anxious and interested spectators. The citizens of the United States cherish sentiments the most friendly in favour of the liberty and happiness of their fellowmen on that side of the Atlantic. In the wars of the European powers in matters relating to themselves, we have never taken any part, nor does it comport with our policy so to do. It is only when our rights are invaded or seriously menaced that we resent injuries or make preparation for our defense. With the movements in this hemisphere we are of necessity more immediately connected, and by causes which must be obvious to all enlightened and impartial observers.

The political system of the allied powers is essentially different in this respect from that of America. This difference proceeds from that which exists in their respective governments; and to the defence of our own, which has been achieved by the loss of so much blood and treasure, and matured by the wisdom of their most enlightened citizens, and under which we have enjoyed unexampled felicity, this whole nation is devoted. We owe it, therefore, to candour and to the amicable relations existing between the United States and those powers to declare that we should consider any attempt on their part to extend their system to any portion of this hemisphere as dangerous to our peace and safety. With the existing colonies or dependencies of any European power we have not interfered and shall not interfere. But with the governments who have declared their independence and maintained it, and whose independence we have, on great consideration and on just principles, acknowledged, we could not view any interposition for the purpose of oppressing them, or controlling in any other manner their destiny, by any European power in any other light than as the manifestation of an unfriendly disposition toward the United States. In the war between those new governments and Spain, we declared our neutrality at the time of their recognition, and to this we have adhered, and shall continue to adhere, provided no change shall occur which, in the judgment of the competent authorities of this government, shall make a corresponding change on the part of the United States indispensable to their security.

The late events in Spain and Portugal show that Europe is still unsettled. Of this important fact, no stronger proof can be adduced than that the allied powers should have thought it proper, on any principle satisfactory to themselves, to have interposed by force in the internal concerns of Spain. To what extent such interposition may be carried, on the same principle, is a question in which all independent powers whose governments differ from theirs are interested, even those most remote, and surely none more so than the United States. Our policy in regard to Europe, which was adopted at an early stage of the wars which have so long agitated that quarter of the globe, nevertheless remains the same, which is, not to interfere in the internal concerns of any of its powers; to consider the government de facto as the legitimate government for us; to cultivate friendly relations with it, and to preserve those relations by a frank, firm, and manly policy, meeting in all instances the just claims of every power, submitting to injuries from none. But in regard to those continents, circumstances are eminently and conspicuously different. It is impossible that the allied powers should extend their political system to any portion of either continent without endangering our peace and happiness; nor can anyone believe that our southern brethren, if [left] to themselves, would adopt it of their own accord. It is equally impossible, therefore, that we should behold such interposition in any form with indifference. If we look to the comparative strength and resources of Spain and those new governments, and their distance from each other, it must be obvious that she can never subdue them. It is still the true policy of the United States to leave the parties to themselves, in the hope that other powers will pursue the same course.

32. NAPOLEAN-I [BONAPARTE] (1769–1821)

Napoleon I was a French emperor and general whose brilliant victories over Austrians and Russians made him practically the master of Europe.
The following speech was addressed to his soldiers on 27 March 1796 when entering Italy.

Soldiers, you are naked and ill-fed. Government owes you much and can give you nothing. The patience and courage you have shown in the midst of this rocky wilderness are admirable; but they gain you no renown; no glory results to you from your endurance. It is my design to lead you into the most fertile plains of the world. Rich provinces and great cities will be in your power. There you will find honour, glory, and wealth. Soldiers of Italy, will you be wanting in courage or perseverance?

Soldiers, you have rushed like a torrent from the top of the Apennines. You have overthrown and scattered all that opposed your march. Piedmont, delivered from Austrian tyranny, indulges her natural sentiments of peace and friendship toward France. Milan is yours, and the republican flag waves throughout Lombardy. The Dukes of Parma and Medona owe their political existence to your generosity alone.

The army which so proudly threatened you can find no barrier to protect it against your courage; neither the Po, the Ticino, nor the Adda could stop you for a single day. These vaunted bulwarks of Italy opposed you in vain; you passed them as rapidly as the Apennines.

These great successes have filled the heart of your country with joy. Your representatives have ordered a festival to commemorate your victories, which has been held in every district of the republic. There your fathers, your wives, sisters, and mistresses rejoined in your good fortune and proudly boasted of belonging to you.

Yes, soldiers, you have done much. But remains there nothing more to do? Shall it be said of us that we have conquered, but not now to make use of victory? Shall posterity reproach us with having found Capua in Lombardy? But I see you already hasten to arms. An effeminate response is tedious to you; the days which are lost to glory are lost to your happiness. Well, then, let us set forth! We have still forced marches to make, enemies to subdue, laurels to gather, injuries to revenge. Let those who have sharpened the daggers of civil war in France, who have dared to murder our ministers and burnt our ships at Toulon tremble!

The hour of vengeance has struck; but let the people of all countries be free from apprehension; we are the friends of the people everywhere, and of those great men whom we have taken for our models. To restore the capital, to replace the statues of the heroes who rendered it illustrious, to rouse the Roman people, stupefied by several ages of slavery—such will be the fruit of our victories. They will form an era for posterity. You will have the immortal glory of changing the face of the finest part of Europe. The French people, free and respected by the whole world, will give to Europe a glorious peace, which will indemnify them for the sacrifices of every kind which for the last six years they have been making. You will then return to your homes and your country. Men will say, as they point you out, "He belongs to the army of Italy."

33. JAWAHARLAL NEHRU (1889–1964)

Pandit Nehru was an Indian national leader and statesman, and the first prime minister of India from 1947 till his death.

This speech 'Tryst wtih Destiny' was delivered in the constituent assembly on 14 August 1947.

*L*ong years ago we made a tryst with destiny, and now the time comes when we shall redeem our pledge, not wholly or in full measure, but very substantially. At the stroke of the midnight hour, when the world sleeps, India will awake to life and freedom. A moment comes, which comes but rarely in history, when we step out from the old to the new, when an age ends, and when the soul of a nation, long suppressed, finds utterance. It is fitting that at this solemn moment we take the pledge of dedication to the service of India and her people and to the still larger cause of humanity.

At the dawn of history, India started on her unending quest, and trackless centuries are filled with her striving and the grandeur of her success and her failures. Through good and ill fortune alike she has never lost sight of that quest or forgotten the ideals which gave her strength. We end today a period of ill fortune and India discovers herself again. The achievement we celebrate today is but a step, an opening of opportunity, to the greater triumphs and achievement that awaits us. Are we brave enough and wise enough to grasp this opportunity and accept the challenge of the future?

Freedom and power bring responsibility. The responsibility rests upon this assembly, a sovereign body representing the sovereign people of India. Before the birth of freedom we have endured all the pains of labour and our hearts are heavy with the memory of this sorrow. Some of those pains continue even now.

Nevertheless, the sorrow is over and it is the future that beckons to us now.

That future is not one of ease today but of incessant striving so that we may fulfil the pledges we have so often meant—the service of the millions who suffer. It means the ending of poverty and ignorance and disease and inequality of opportunity. The ambition of the greatest man of our generation has been to wipe every tear from every eye. That may be beyond us, but as long as there are tears and suffering, so long our work will not be over.

And so we have to labour and to work, and work hard, to give reality to our dreams. Those dreams are for India, but they are also for the world, for all the nations and peoples are too closely knit together today for any one of them to imagine that it can live apart. Peace has been said to be indivisible; so is freedom. It is prosperity now, and so also is disaster in this one world that can no longer be split into isolated fragments.

To the people of India, wise representatives as we are, we make an appeal to join us with faith and confidence in this great adventure. This is no time for petty and destructive criticism, no time for ill will or blaming others. We have to build the noble mansion of free India where all her children may dwell.

I beg to move, Sir, that it be resolved that after the last stroke of midnight, all members of the Constituent Assembly present on this occasion, do take the following pledge:

At this solemn moment when the people of India, through suffering and sacrifice, have secured freedom, I,......, member of the Constituent Assembly of India, do dedicate myself in all humility to the service of India and her people to the end that this ancient land attain her rightful place in the world and make her full and willing contribution to the promotion of world peace and the welfare of mankind.

34. RICHARD NIXON (1913–1994)

*Richard Milhous Nixon was the Republican president of the US
from 1969 to 1974.
The following is his inaugural address on 20 January 1969, on
assuming office.*

Senator Dirksen, Mr Chief Justice, Mr Vice President, President
Johnson, Vice President Humphrey, my fellow Americans, and
my fellow citizens of the world community:

I ask you to share with me today the majesty of this moment.
In the orderly transfer of power, we celebrate the unity that keeps
us free. Each moment in history is a fleeting time, precious and
unique. But some stand out as moments of beginning, in which
courses are set that shape decades or centuries. This can be such
a moment.

Forces now are converging that make possible, for the first
time, the hope that many of man's deepest aspirations can at last
be realized. The spiraling pace of change allows us to contemplate,
within our own lifetime, advances that once would have taken
centuries. In throwing wide the horizons of space, we have
discovered new horizons on earth.

The second third of this century has been a time of proud
achievement. We have made enormous strides in science and
industry and agriculture. We have shared our wealth more
broadly than ever. We have learned at last to manage a modern
economy to assure its continued growth. We have given freedom
new reach, and we have begun to make its promise real for black
as well as for white.

We see the hope of tomorrow in the youth of today. I know
America's youth. I believe in them. We can be proud that they
are better educated, more committed, more passionately driven

by conscience than any generation in our history. No people has ever been so close to the achievement of a just and abundant society, or so possessed of the will to achieve it. Because our strengths are so great, we can afford to appraise our weaknesses with candor and to approach them with hope.

In pursuing our goals of full employment, better housing, excellence in education; in rebuilding our cities and improving our rural areas; in protecting our environment and enhancing the quality of life—in all these and more, we will and must press urgently forward.

To match the magnitude of our tasks, we need the energies of our people—enlisted not only in grand enterprises, but more importantly in those small, splendid efforts that make headlines in the neighborhood newspaper instead of the national journal. With these, we can build a great cathedral of the spirit—each of us raising it one stone at a time, as he reaches out to his neighbour, helping, caring, doing.

As we learn to go forward together at home, let us also seek to go forward together with all mankind. Let us take as our goal—where peace is unknown, make it welcome; where peace is fragile, make it strong; where peace is temporary, make it permanent. After a period of confrontation, we are entering an era of negotiation. Let all nations know that during this administration, our lines of communication will be open.

Over the past twenty years, since I first came to this capital as a freshman Congressman, I have visited most of the nations of the world. I have come to know the leaders of the world, and the great forces, the hatreds, the fears that divide the world. I know that peace does not come through wishing for it, that there is no substitute for days and even years of patient and prolonged diplomacy. I also know the people of the world. I have seen the hunger of a homeless child, the pain of a man wounded in battle, the grief of a mother who has lost her son. I know these have no ideology, no race. I know America. I know the heart of America is good.

I speak from my own heart, and the heart of my country, the deep concern we have for those who suffer, and those who sorrow. I have taken an oath today in the presence of God and my countrymen to uphold and defend the Constitution of the United States. To that oath I now add this sacred commitment: I shall consecrate my office, my energies, and all the wisdom I can summon, to the cause of peace among nations. Let this message be heard by strong and weak alike.

We have endured a long night of the American spirit. But as our eyes catch the dimness of the first rays of dawn, let us not curse the remaining dark. Let us gather the light. Our destiny offers, not the cup of despair, but the chalice of opportunity. So let us seize it, not in fear, but in gladness and, "riders on the earth together," let us go forward, firm in our faith, steadfast in our purpose, cautious of the dangers; but sustained by our confidence in the will of God and the promise of man.

35. GENERAL GEORGE S PATTON (1885–1945)

George Smith Patton was the most successful US field commander in World War II.

The following is the final pep-talk speech that he gave in England on 17 May 1944.

en, this stuff some sources sling around about America wanting to stay out of the war and not wanting to fight is a lot of baloney! Americans love to fight, traditionally. All real Americans love the sting and clash of battle. America loves a winner. America will not tolerate a loser. Americans despise a coward; Americans play to win. That's why America has never lost and never will lose a war.

You are not all going to die. Only two per cent of you, right here today, would be killed in a major battle.

Death must not be feared. Death, in time, comes to all of us. And every man is scared in his first action. If he says he's not, he's a goddamn liar. Some men are cowards, yes, but they fight just the same, or get the hell slammed out of them.

The real hero is the man who fights even though he's scared. Some get over their fright in a minute, under fire; others take an hour; for some it takes days; but a real man will never let the fear of death overpower his honour, his sense of duty, to his country and to his manhood.

All through your army careers, you've been bitching about what you call chicken-shit drills. That, like everything else in the army, has a definite purpose. That purpose is instant obedience to orders and to create and maintain constant alertness! This must be bred into every soldier. A man must be alert all the time if he expects to stay alive. If not, some German son-of-a-bitch will sneak up behind him with a sock full of shit! There are four hundred neatly marked graves somewhere in Sicily, all because one man went to sleep on his job — but they are German graves, because we caught the bastards asleep!

An army is a team — lives, sleeps, fights, and eats as a team. This individual hero stuff is a lot of horse shit! The bilious bastards who write that kind of stuff for the *Saturday Evening Post* don't know any more about real fighting under fire than they know about fucking! Every single man in the Army plays a vital role. Every man has his job to do and must do it. What if every truck driver decided that he didn't like the whine of a shell overhead, turned yellow and jumped headlong into a ditch? What if every man thought, "They won't miss me, just one in millions?" Where in hell would we be now? Where would our country, our loved ones, our homes, even the world, be?

No, thank God, Americans don't think like that. Every man does his job, serves the whole. Ordnance men supply and maintain the guns and vast machinery of this war, to keep us rolling. Quartermasters bring up clothes and food, for where we're going, there isn't a hell of a lot to steal. Every last man on KP has a job to do, even the guy who boils the water to keep us from getting the GI shits!

Remember, men, you don't know I'm here. No mention of that is to be made in any letters. The USA is supposed to be wondering what the hell has happened to me. I'm not supposed to be commanding this Army, I'm not supposed even to be in England. Let the first bastards to find out be the goddamn Germans. I want them to look up and howl, "Ach, it's the goddamn Third Army and that son-of-a-bitch Patton again!"

We want to get this thing over and get the hell out of here, and get at those purple-pissin' Japs!!! The shortest road home is through Berlin and Tokyo! We'll win this war, but we'll win it only by showing the enemy we have more guts than they have or ever will have!

There's one great thing you men can say when it's all over and you're home once more. You can thank God that twenty years from now, when you're sitting around the fireside with your grandson on your knee and he asks you what you did in the war, you won't have to shift him to the other knee, cough, and say, "I shovelled shit in Louisiana."

36. POPE JOHN PAUL II (1920–2005)

Pope John Paul was the first non-Italian pope in 455 years. He was Polish.

In March 2000, he visited Yad Vashem in Jerusalem to pay tribute to the six million Jews killed by the Nazis from 1938 onwards. This speech was made there at Israel's main Holocaust Memorial.

The words of the ancient Psalm, rise from our hearts: I have become like a broken vessel. I hear the whispering of many — terror on every side — as they scheme together against me, as they plot to take my life. But I trust in you, O Lord: I say, you are my God. (*Psalms 31:13-15*)

In this place of memories, the mind and heart and soul feel an extreme need for silence. Silence in which to remember. Silence in which to try to make some sense of the memories which come flooding back. Silence because there are no words strong enough to deplore the terrible tragedy of the Shoah.

My own personal memories are of all that happened when the Nazis occupied Poland during the war. I remember my Jewish friends and neighbours, some of whom perished, while others survived. I have come to Yad Vashem to pay homage to the millions of Jewish people who, stripped of everything, especially of human dignity, were murdered in the Holocaust. More than half a century has passed, but the memories remain.

Here, as at Auschwitz and many other places in Europe, we are overcome by the echo of the heart-rending laments of so many. Men, women and children, cry out to us from the depths of the horror that they knew. How can we fail to heed their cry? No one can forget or ignore what happened. No one can diminish its scale.

We wish to remember. But we wish to remember for a purpose, namely to ensure that never again will evil prevail, as it did for the millions of innocent victims of Nazism. How could man have such utter contempt for man? Because he had reached the point of contempt for God. Only a godless ideology could plan and carry out the extermination of a whole people.

The honour given to the 'Just Gentiles' by the state of Israel at Yad Vashem for having acted heroically to save Jews, sometimes to the point of giving their own lives, is a recognition that not even in the darkest hour is every light extinguished. That is why the *Psalms* and the entire *Bible*, though well aware of the human capacity for evil, also proclaims that evil will not have the last word.

Out of the depths of pain and sorrow, the believer's heart cries out: I trust in you, O Lord. I say, you are my God. (*Psalms 31:14*) Jews and Christians share an immense spiritual patrimony, flowing from God's self-revelation. Our religious teachings and our spiritual experience demand that we overcome evil with good. We remember, but not with any desire for vengeance or as an incentive to hatred. For us, to remember is to pray for peace and justice, and to commit ourselves to their cause. Only a world at peace, with justice for all, can avoid repeating the mistakes and terrible crimes of the past.

As bishop of Rome and successor of the Apostle Peter, I assure the Jewish people that the Catholic Church, motivated by the Gospel law of truth and love, and by no political considerations, is deeply saddened by the hatred, acts of persecution and displays of anti-Semitism directed against the Jews by Christians at any time and in any place. The church rejects racism in any form as a denial of the image of the Creator inherent in every human being.

In this place of solemn remembrance, I fervently pray that our sorrow for the tragedy which the Jewish people suffered in the twentieth century will lead to a new relationship between Christians and Jews. Let us build a new future in which there will be no more anti-Jewish feeling among Christians or anti-Christian feeling among Jews, but rather the mutual respect required of those who adore the one Creator and Lord, and look to Abraham as our common father in faith.

The world must heed the warning that comes to us from the victims of the Holocaust, and from the testimony of the survivors. Here at Yad Vashem the memory lives on, and burns itself onto

our souls. It makes us cry out: I hear the whispering of many —
terror on every side — but I trust in you, O Lord. I say, you are
my God. *(Psalms 31:13-15)*

37. RAJENDRA PRASAD (1884–1963)

Dr Prasad was India's first president. He was a statesman and a devout Gandhian.

The following is his address to Parliament on 13 May 1957 on assuming office for a second term.

*Y*ou and the members of the legislatures of the states, chosen by an electorate of nearly two hundred million voters of our country, in accord with our constitutional procedures, have called me once again to the high office of the president of the republic. I am deeply conscious of the honour and I am grateful for the confidence which you have reposed in me. It shall be my endeavour to continue to deserve the trust and the affection of which I have been so long the happy recipient.

It gives me great pleasure to welcome you, as members of the Second Parliament in the history of our Republic. Some of you have been members of one or other of the Houses of Parliament, or come to Parliament with rich experience in your state legislatures. There are others among you who have been elected to Parliament for the first time. All of you will find, in your life and duties as Members of Parliament, both in the legislature and your constituencies, immense and varied opportunities; and fields of constructive work in the service of our country and people. I wish you all good fortune and a very successful tenure of Parliamentary life.

We are in the second year of our Second Five Year Plan. There has been some inevitable slowing down in the first year of the plan, resulting partly from the reorganisation of the states. This imposes a greater strain and calls for added effort both by the government and the people during the remaining period of that plan. My government are fully conscious of this.

The economic situation, more particularly in relation to the plan, confronts us with factors which, while they do not warrant grave apprehension, are matters of serious concern and they are engaging the attention of my ministers. The deficit in the central and state budgets and the strain on our foreign exchange resources occasioned by the requirements of the plan and of industrial development, generally, as well as by external factors, call for determined and planned efforts. They call for both conservation and expansion of our resources by effecting real economies, by planned restrictions on certain imports, by expansion of export trade and by increasing national self-sufficiency both in the fields of industry and agriculture. They will call for savings to be utilised for production and the abandonment of unproductive and antisocial habits of hoarding and speculation. These can only be effectively achieved by efforts and vigilance not only on the part of the Government but by the people as well.

It would be the easier, but not the gainful or constructive way, to bridge the gaps to which I have referred, by halting development. This will, however, provide no real or long-term remedy. Our endeavour has to be to mobilise and conserve resource for greater productivity and for maintaining and improving development. My government are fully aware of the problem and of the effort required. They are equally concerned that our temporary difficulties should not lead us in the direction of retarding progress and development but that the difficulties should be overcome, where necessary, by reconsideration and revision of methods and by planned mobilisation of resources and not by either the abandonment or slowing down of the progress towards our objectives.

Public opinion plays a large and important conclusive part in the success of such endeavour. The determination and fervour of our people, their readiness to accept discipline, to respond to the call for efforts and their resolve not to be led into antisocial behaviour, such as by hoarding or wasteful spending, alone will help the country to pass successfully through the present crucial period of our Second Year Plan.

Members of Parliament, the country looks to you a great deal for that sustained and special effort in support of the policies and endeavours which my government will initiate in this behalf, which help us to surmount difficulties and to achieve success.

While food production has increased, and the increases have been maintained except for the results of natural calamities, more especially in certain parts of Bihar and the eastern districts of Uttar Pradesh, we have a considerable way to go before our country becomes fully self-sufficient in food. There are signs of slight abatement in the rising trend of food production and improved crop prospects. Except in the case of some of the coarse gains adversely affected by climatic conditions, the crop yields and estimates not only do not indicate a shortfall but have recorded appreciable increases.

My government have also entered into arrangements for necessary imports of foodgrains and for building up reverse, which will prevent price increases and bridge the gaps that still remain. A large storage construction programme has been undertaken. The behaviour of the public is a large and often determining factor in preventing rise in food prices which is often caused by the apprehension of shortages resulting in the resort to hoarding as well as to the tendency to panic. The food situation, thanks to the increased production and the steps taken by my government does not warrant any lack of public confidence in regard to supplies. My government propose to keep Parliament informed of the position in regard to food and the estimates of supply and requirements. It may be hoped that a knowledge of the facts will help to allay needless apprehensions and prevent artificial shortages and higher prices.

My government are happy to state that their decision to lay stress on food production and agriculture, generally, in the Community Project plans has yielded handsome results. The Community Development and the National Extension Service programmes have made great strides. Higher targets in agriculture, health and sanitation have been achieved. The National Sample Survey shows that, at the end of the First Year Plan, the crop yields in the Community Development Projects and National Extension Service Blocks areas were approximately 25 per cent higher than for the country as a whole. The Community Projects and National Extension Blocks now cover 2,22,000 villages.

State undertakings continue to make notable progress and new targets have been reached in almost every enterprise. There has also been expansion in the private sector. Khadi and village

industries will receive a further impetus with the setting-up of
the Khadi and Village Industries Commission as a statutory body.
Among the major new projects that will soon be inaugurated is
the Neyveli Lignite Project where the first mine-cut will be made
this month. My government attach importance to the building up
of a plant for the manufacture of heavy machinery and steps are
being taken to this end.

To reduce the pressure on our resources of foreign exchange,
my government are making efforts to obtain deferred payment
arrangements for major projects. Long term credits for certain
projects are being negotiated.

Consequent on the reorganisation of the states, advisory
committees have set up for the union territories and territorial
councils have been established in Himachal Pradesh, Manipur
and Tripura. A corporation for Delhi will be soon established. A
new union territory of the Lacadives, Minicoy and Amindivi
Islands has come into existence and the Five Year Plan for the
Andamans Islands at a total cost of Rs. 592.50 lakhs will include
the development of communication between the islands and the
mainland.

Shipyard construction and the building of ships of modern
design have made great progress at Vishakhapatnam and plans
for a second shipyard are now in hand.

My government have initiated measures to relieve housing
shortages and promote housing standards, slum clearance and
Plantation Housing Schemes and housing for low income groups
and subsidised industrial housing. An urgent requirement of Delhi
and the other big cities of India is the clearance of slum areas,
and this problem is receiving the consideration of the central and
state governments and the corporations concerned.

Two ordinances have promulgated since the last session of
Parliament. Bills dealing with these ordinances will be placed
before Parliament. These are:

i) The Life Insurance Corporation (Amendment) Ordinance,
   1957.

ii) The Industrial Disputes (Amendment) Ordinance, 1957.

My government will also submit to Parliament a number of
other bills during the current session.

An interim statement of revenue and expenditure for 1957–
58 was presented to Parliament during its last session and votes

on account authorising expenditure for a part of the year were passed. That statement of revenue and expenditure will be presented again to Parliament in this session with such changes as are considered necessary, and Parliament will be asked to approve funds for the whole year.

Our relations with foreign countries continue to be friendly. I addressed Parliament last, we have had the pleasure of receiving as the guests of the Republic, Mr Jozef Cyrankiewicz, prime minister of Poland, Dr Heinrich Von Brentano, foreign minister of the Federal German Republic and Mr Oscaldo Sainte Marie, foreign minister of Chile.

My prime minister will attend the meeting of Commonwealth prime ministers in London at the end of June. During his absence abroad, he will take the opportunity of visiting Syria, Denmark, Finland, Norway, Sweden, the Netherlands, Egypt and Sudan.

While the situation in the Middle East continues to be unsatisfactory and charged with tension, it is a matter of gratification that the Suez Canal has been reopened for navigation. My government welcomes the Declaration made by the Government of Egypt, prior to the opening of the Canal, which reaffirms the convention of 1888 and the determination of Egypt to continue to abide by the principles of the Charter of the United Nations and of International Law. The Declaration provides for the reference of disputes arising from interpretations of the convention and its application as well as certain other matters to the World Court and also to abide by its decisions. The main provisions in the Declaration are, in the view of my government, reasonable and adequate to safeguard the legitimate interests of the world community, if they are worked in a spirit of cooperation and mutual understanding by all concerned. A notable feature of the Declaration is that, while it is made by the Government of Egypt, that government has declared that it has the status of an international instrument and this has been registered with the United Nations. My government feel that this Declaration and its status as an international instrument is a notable contribution to the lowering of tensions in that area and will provide a solution of the difficulties that followed the nationalisation of the Suez Canal.

Dr Gunnar Jarring, a former President of the Security Council, visited Pakistan and India in pursuance of a resolution passed by the Security Council on the 21st of February this year at the end of the debate on Kashmir. Dr Jarring visited India twice and conferred with my prime minister. He has submitted a report to the Security Council.

The subcommittee of the Disarmament Commission has been sitting in London for sometime, but no agreement appears to have been reached on any aspect of disarmament, including the suspension of explosions of nuclear and thermonuclear weapons. The proposals of my government in regard to disarmament were once again referred by the General Assembly of the United Nations at the last session, along with all other proposals, to the Disarmament Commission.

Meanwhile the United States, the Soviet Union, and now the United Kingdom continue their experiments to explode these weapons of mass destruction. World opinion is increasingly concerned about the harmful effect of radiation which has been increasingly and more frequently felt in various parts of the world. The demand for the suspension of these explosions is widespread and continues to the impressed upon the nuclear powers, but hitherto without success.

My Government do not consider that the compromise proposals suggested from diverse quarters for the so-called limitation of these explosions or for their registration will ever rid the world of their harmful effects, or open the way to the abandonment of these weapons of mass destruction. On the other hand, such regularisation of these tests tends to make thermonuclear war legitimate and as having the sanction of the world community. Reports of experiments with more and more deadly weapons of war continue to be received. It is, however, a matter of some gratification that the volume of world opinion against the continuance of experiments has reached a higher level that ever before. My prime minister in a statement before the Lok Sabha in April 1954 put forward for consideration the proposal for a standstill agreement to suspend these explosions. These proposals have since gained much support and the movement of world opinion in favour of it has gathered influence with other nations and in the counsels of the world to bring about the abandonment of these test explosions and the prohibition of nuclear and thermonuclear weapons.

We meet here today one hundred years after the great rising which began in Meerut and spread over considerable parts of India. That was the first major challenge to foreign rule and threw up notable figures, famous in India's history. The uprising was cruelly suppressed, but the spirit of freedom and the desire to be free from foreign domination continued and found expression on many subsequent occasions. Ultimately it led to a great national movement which followed peaceful methods and succeeded in achieving the independence of India. Quite many people gave their lives or otherwise suffered so that India may be free.

India has been independent for nearly ten years now, and during this period Parliament has laboured for the well-being and advancement of this country and her people and for peace and cooperation in the world. These labours have produced substantial results which we see all round us in the country. The progress we have made during these years in our own land has produced in our people hope and self-reliance. This is a substantial foundation on which we can build for the future.

Abroad, my government have striven strenuously to help solve existing tensions in the world and to serve the cause of peace. The country has also accepted heavy responsibilities in the pursuit of this policy, in regard to maintaining the independence of its approach as well as in making contributions to the maintenance of peace, as in Korea, Indo-China and now in the Middle-East.

The tasks that confront us both at home and abroad are not only considerable but at times appear overwhelming. But these tasks have to be faced, difficulties surmounted and objectives achieved if the fruits of independence are to be ensured to our people and if we are to help the world to stop spreading the continual stress and horror of impending catastrophe.

My government will continue their strenuous endeavours in all these directions, to the best of their capacity, conscious of the confidence reposed in them by the country and fortified by the conviction that despite clouds of war, and even despair, the desire for survival and progress is inherent in humanity. Our capacities and resources are limited and our voice in the world may be but small. But neither our national interests, nor our history and traditions, nor our convictions chart any other course for us. Happily for us, this is the common aim and the firm desire of all our people.

38. DR SARVEPALLI RADHAKRISHNAN
(1888–1975)

Dr Radhakrishnan was an Indian scholar, philosopher, writer and statesman. He was the first vice-president and second president of India.

This speech is his address at the Marian Congress in Mumbai on 4 December 1954.

*M*ay I, at the outset, offer you, Cardinal Gracias, our warm congratulations on your appointment as Papal Legate?

I am happy to be here and take part in this ceremony, convinced as I am that the great need of our age is revival of spiritual values. The two wars in our generation and the alarming advances in nuclear weapons, the social strains and upheavals that have become chronic, the lack of any clear vision of the future have had vastly disintegrating effects on our minds and morals.

Many observations are made on the place of religion in modern life, and it is said that it imposes shackles on the human mind, that it blinds reason, that it deadens sensibility, that it asks us to surrender our integrity and submit unthinkingly to authority in belief and practice. Socially, it is argued that it disdains the world, that, if it takes interest in it, it is only to defend the status quo and justify existing wrongs and evils. The leaders of religions are doing little to check the process of decivilising men in the name of vast organisations, of destroying the springs of tenderness, of compassion, of fellow-feeling in the human heart. The need of the world today is human unity and religions are proving to be great obstacles in its way. They have departed from their original purity, lost their dynamic vigour and degenerated into arrogant sects. The spiritual inspiration is buried under irrational habits and mechanical practices.

It is therefore most appropriate that you should have selected for the motto of this Congress the seventh verse of the first chapter of the second epistle of Paul, the Apostle of Timothy: 'The spirit he has bestowed on us is not one that shrinks form danger; it is a spirit of action, of love and of discipline.'

Freedom from fear, *abhaya*, which does not shrink from danger, a state of peace and power — this is the inward grace of a religious mind; its social expression is action and love. Love of God and love of neighbour are the two sides, inward and outward, of a truly religious soul.

Love of God is not a mere phrase, not an intellectual proposition to which we consent with our minds. It is a transforming experience, a burning conviction. Life eternal cannot be had from mere knowledge of the meaning of texts. It is the workship of God in spirit and in truth. It is what is called *dvitiyam janma*, a second birth. We are born into the world of nature and necessity, of darkness and death; we must be reborn into the world of spirit and freedom, of light and life. The destiny of man is not natural perfection, but it is life in God. Human nature finds its fulfilment in God.

Religion, in all its forms, declares that the human being should be made into a new man. Man, as he is, is the raw material for an inward growth, an inner evolution. As he is, he is incomplete, unfinished, imperfect. He has to reach inner completion through meta-noia which is not adequately translated as repentance. Unless, in Jesus's words, we repent, unless we are reborn, unless we are renewed in our consciousness, unless we become like a little child, responsive to the magic and mystery of the world, we cannot enter the kingdom of God. When a man is reborn in the world of spirit, gains insight into reality, his lostness is no more. His loneliness disappears and he has communion with the Divine.

Discipline of human nature is essential for the attainment of the goal. Purity of mind and body is the means for perfection. Models of purity, as the one you are celebrating this year, help us to purify ourselves. Peace of mind can be attained only by self-control, the control of our emotions and desires.

Such a redeemed soul participates in the work of the world: *Seva-dharma-karma-vimukhah krsna krsneti vadinah te harer dvesino mudhah dharmartham janma yadd hareh.*

Those who merely say "Krishna" and are indifferent to their respective duties are enemies of God, foolish, for the very Lord takes birth for the sake of righteousness. God is not merely justice and power; He is love and understanding. If we are to imitate the Divine, we must work for the betterment of the world, in spite of pettiness and defeat, treachery and disappointment, despite death itself. The authentic religious soul feels that it is better to live in accord with the ideals of truth and love than retreat into cynicism, denial and despair. Even when misfortunes befall us, we should not shrink from danger but be 'steady like a lamp in a windless place' — *Bhagavad Gita*; or as Dante puts it, 'stand like a tower whose summit never shakes'. Jackals may howl in the field, but up above shine the stars. Goodness is more deeply rooted in the nature of things than its opposite. Life has a destiny which justifies any sacrifices to which it is called.

All our activities, whether they relate to our society or the world, should be permeated by the spirit of religion. When we know what a frightful evil war would be in this atomic age, it is our religious duty to do everything in our power to avert it. The world is not for hate and malice, for revenge and destruction. We must stand up for the spirit of just and merciful dealing and work for love and charity on earth. If the brotherhood of peoples is to be realised, all nations must go through a process of inner renewal.

On the 23rd of November I had the honour of a private audience with Pope Pius XII whose purity of life and penetration of mind are well-known.

He has issued a prayer for the year, which asks us to strive for peace and fellowship.

Convert the wicked, dry the tears of the afflicted and oppressed, comfort the poor and humble, quench hatreds, sweeten harshness, safeguard the flower of purity in youth, make all men feel the attraction of goodness. May they recognise that they are brothers and that the nations are members of one family upon which may there shine forth the sun of a universal and sincere peace.

Religion is the force which can bring about this inward renewal. The different religions are the windows through which God's light shines into man's soul. There can be differences about the rays they transmit or the intensity of their splendour, but these differences do not justify discords and rivalries. We must distinguish between the eternal light and its temporal reflections. The followers of different religions are partners in one spiritual quest, pursuing alternative approaches to the goal of spiritual life, the vision of God. It is this view that has been adopted by this country from ancient times. We have here Jews, Christians, Catholics and Protestants, Parsees, Hindus, Muslims, who are exhorted by the spirit of this country which is incorporated in our Constitution, to learn from one another. May this Congress contribute to the process of cooperation among the different religions and further the spirit of spiritual understanding and religious enlightenment and fellowship!

39. SHEIKH MUJIBUR RAHMAN (1920–1975)

Mujibur Rahman was the father of the new nation of Bangladesh, and its president and prime minister.

He addressed a mammoth rally on 7 March 1971 at the Race Course in Dhaka.

Struggle this time is the struggle for independence.

Today I come to you with a heavy heart. You know everything and understand as well. We tried our best. But the streets of Dhaka, Chittagong, Khulna, Rajshiahi and Rangpur have been dyed red with the blood of our brethren.

People of Bangladesh today want liberation. They want to survive. They want to have their rights. What wrong did we do? In the elections, people of Bangladesh voted for me and the Awami League. We had a hope that we would sit in the assembly and frame a constitution which would lead to the emancipation of the people economically, politically and culturally.

But today we are sorry to say that the history of the 23 years is the history of the dying cries of the people of Bangladesh, the history of pathetic bloodshed and the history of dyeing the streets with the blood of the people of this country. We shed blood in 1952. We could not establish ourselves in power in 1954 even after winning the elections. In 1958 Ayub Khan promulgated the martial law in the country and made us slaves for 10 years. In 1966 the six-point programme was launched and, only for that, many of my brothers were shot to death. Ayub had to step down in the face of a mass upsurge in 1979, and then came Yahya Khan. He said he would return power to the people and let the country have a constitution. We believed in his words.

What happened after that, all of you know. The elections were held. I had talks with President Yahya Khan and requested him, as the leader of the majority party not only in Bangladesh but in the whole of Pakistan as well, to convene the National Assembly on February 15. But he did not listen to my proposal. He listened to the words of Mr. Bhutto. Mr. Bhutto proposed to convene the session in the first week of March. I said, all right. We will sit in the Assembly and though we are the majority, we will accept any just proposal even if it comes from a lone member. Mr. Bhutto came to Dhaka. I had talks with him. He said the doors of discussion were not closed; there would be further talks. Also came other West Pakistani leaders of various parties in the Parliament and we had talks with them as well. Our aim was to frame a constitution after having discussions.

But Mr. Bhutto said that the Assembly would turn into a 'slaughter' house should the West Pakistani members come here. He threatened to liquidate anyone who tried to join the Assembly from West Pakistan. He would launch a movement from Peshawar to Karachi. Not even a shop would be allowed to open. I said, the Assembly would sit. But the session was postponed on March 1.

Yahya Khan summoned the assembly as president. I said I will go to the Assembly. Mr. Bhutto said he won't; 35 members came from West Pakistan. But suddenly it was postponed. The blame was put on the people of Bangladesh and on me.

The people of Bangladesh raised their voice in protest against this move. I urged the people to observe peaceful *hartal*. I asked them to close down all factories and mills. The people responded. They came out on the streets on their own and resolved to continue the movement.

But what did we get in return? Arms were used against the unarmed people of Bangladesh. The arms which were bought by our money, to safeguard the country from foreign aggression, are now being used to kill our poor people. My distressed people are being shot at.

We are the majority in Pakistan. Whenever we, the Bangalees, wanted to take over power, wanted to become masters of our own destiny, they pounced on us—every time.

Yahya Khan has said that I agreed to attend the Round Table Conference of March 10. In fact spoke to him over the telephone. I told him: you are the President of the country. Please come to Dhaka and see for yourself how my poor people have been killed, how the laps of my mothers have been emptied. Please come, see and then decide for yourself. I had categorically said that there would be no RTC or anything of that sort. What RTC? How can I sit across the same table with those who have taken blood of my people?

In his speech which was made without consulting me or my men, but after having a long secret talk for five hours, Yahya Khan has put all the blame on me and the people of Bengal. I have categorically said, the struggle this time is the struggle for freedom; the struggle this time is the struggle for independence. The president has convened the assembly on 25th March. But the bloodstains have not yet dried up. I want to make it clear that Sheikh Mujibur Rahman cannot go to the RTC stepping over the bloodshed by the martyrs.

Before we go to the Assembly, our demands have to be conceded. The first demand: the martial law has to be withdrawn. Second, the army has to go back to the barracks. Third, power has to be transferred to the elected representatives of the people. And fourth, official enquiries have to be made about the recent killings. After that we will consider whether we can sit in the Assembly or not. The question of attending the Assembly does not arise at all before these demands are met. Our people have not authorised us to do so.

My brothers, do you have faith in me? I do not want to be the prime minister. I want the rights of the people. They could not buy me by offering the prime ministership. They could not buy me on point of death-by-hanging. You freed me from the conspiracy case by shedding your blood. I promised that day, on this very Race Course, that I would repay the loan of blood—by blood. Do you remember that? This day too, I am as ready as before.

I would like to declare that from today all lower courts, high court, the Supreme Court, offices and educational institutions will remain closed for an indefinite period of time. The poor people should not suffer. Rickshaw, cart, train and launch would ply. Only Secretariat, Supreme Court, High Court, Judge's Court, Semi-Government offices, WAPDA, etc., would not function.

You should go to draw your salaries on the appointed day. If the salaries are not paid and if another single bullet is fired and my people are killed, I would urge you to make every home a fortress. You will have to face the enemy with whatever you have. You should block all their roads. If I am not here to direct you, you should continue the movement.

Even now I say to the soldiers that you are our brothers. Stay inside your barracks and nobody will say a word to you. But if you open fire again, things will go wrong. You cannot silence seventy-five million people anymore. Remember, once we have learnt how to face death, nobody will be able to suppress us.

Awami League has formed a Relief Committee for helping the families of the martyrs and injured persons. We shall try to help them. Please contribute to this fund as much as you can. I request the mill owners to pay full salaries to the workers who participated in the week-long hartal.

I ask the government employees to obey what I say. Make sure that nobody is seen in the offices. Realisation of taxes will remain suspended until this land is liberated. But I urge upon you—you are our brothers. Don't push the country to total destruction. If there is an amicable settlement of the problem, there is still a chance of our living together as brothers.

But be careful of one thing. The enemy has entered our own ranks. They are trying to create differences among ourselves, and organise looting and other such activities. The seventy-five million people—Hindu, Muslim or Bengalee, non-Bengalee—all are our brothers. It is our duty to protect them.

If the radio does not broadcast our words, no Bengalee should go to the radio station. If the TV does not telecast our news, no Bengalee should go to the TV station. The banks will remain open for two hours so that people can draw their salary. No money could be transferred from East Bengal to West Pakistan. Telephone and telegram will operate within East Bengal and news could be transmitted to foreign counties.

I request you to form action committees in every village, ward and union under the leadership of the Awami League. Prepare yourself with whatever you have. Remember, once we have shed our blood, we will not hesitate to shed more. But we will free the people of this country, Insha Allah! The struggle this time is the struggle for freedom; the struggle this time is the struggle for independence.

Joi Bangla!

40. P V NARASIMHA RAO (1921–2005)

Narasimha Rao was the prime minister of India from 1991 to 1996. The following is the Gandhi Memorial Address at the UNESCO, delivered in Paris on 12 June 1995.

*F*riends, whether it was the liberation struggles against the colonial regimes, non-alignment, nuclear disarmament, wealth generation and distribution, consumerism and eco-friendly development, the content and range of the ideas expressed by the Mahatma, no less than his translation of those ideas into practice were remarkable in many ways.

My today's address here has its origin in the decision of the General Council of UNESCO in 1993 to commemorate the 125th anniversary of Gandhi as a great world personality whose thoughts and creative modes of non-violence shaped socioeconomic and political currents in the twentieth century.

What are the likely, possible and desirable arenas of *satyagrahi* action in our times? Since we are located in an age when the complete annihilation of human civilisation through weapons of mass destruction continues to be a possibility, it is relevant to ask whether the Mahatma's concept of conflict resolution has any role to play in relations between sovereign nations as well as those between different sections within the states.

At the risk of touching upon a theme which may appear parochial yet has a worldwide potential that needs to be explored, I would contend that the Gandhian sense of power profoundly influenced the foreign policy of India after independence in 1947.

This policy, as is well-known, sought to bring together the newly liberated nations of Asia, Africa and Latin America — with their common memory of domination — on a common platform to confer self-confidence upon polities which lacked the sinews of conventional strength in the post-World War II era.

As classically formulated, non-alignment probably assumes a different significance from the one it had in the third quarter of our century. But as a principle of equity and sanity, which enabled the developing nations to speak with a voice of dignity in the fora of the world, non-alignment is as relevant today as it was when it was enunciated.

Although the non-aligned movement took shape in 1962, the concept predates Indian independence. The principle was clearly enunciated in a resolution of the working committee of the Indian National Congress in 1946.

Yet, in relating Gandhian principles to the conduct of world affairs, I want to go beyond non-alignment, to touch upon the vital issue of nuclear disarmament in our times. Indeed, our deep commitment to Gandhian values, as a nation which looks up to the Mahatma as its most eminent citizen in the twentieth century, is eloquently reflected in the proposal which we initiated in 1988 for a phased and universal programme of nuclear disarmament.

Rajiv Gandhi articulated this vision of 'rid the world of nuclear weapons' at the special session of the UN General Assembly on disarmament. As heirs to Mahatma Gandhi, we look upon our proposal for universal nuclear disarmament as Gandhian in spirit, just as we look upon it as a measure which can make the world a safer place for generations to come. Since UNESCO is dedicated to the promotion of world peace, I take this opportunity to reiterate the outline of this essentially Gandhian proposal for universal nuclear disarmament. I commend this proposal before these assembled men and women of scholarship in the conviction that they will so influence world opinion that the dream of universal nuclear disarmament will became a reality within a definite stipulated time.

The question of nuclear disarmament is only one of the issues on the agenda of *satyagrahi* action in our times. No less significance relating to the generation of wealth between and within nations in the world community; or questions pertaining to the articulation of local and regional identities within existing polities; and finally, to the vulnerability of the nation-state itself, in the face of emerging supranational regional organisations and changing technological and information system. I shall touch upon these problems separately, with a view to locating them within the Gandhian discourse. I shall also try to draw from the Gandhian discourse possible lines of solution to these problems.

Perhaps it would be appropriate to dwell upon the questions of wealth generation and its distribution in the first instance. There is a widespread yet erroneous belief, within India as well as outside India, that Gandhi lacked a full understanding of industrial societies; and that he may have been dismissive about the increasing pace and impact of industrialisation in the twentieth century. Nothing could be further from the truth. As a student of law in London, Gandhi explored industrialisation in Great Britain intensively and set out his understanding of this phenomenon in a work called *Hind Swaraj*. The Mahatma's quarrel was not with industrialisation as such but with situations which reduced human beings to helpless instruments of technology in the name of development. This de-humanisation was anathema to Gandhi, whether it emanated in the capitalist system or in the communist system. I still remember how Gandhi was condemned in both camps, whatever may be the encomiums he is earning after he died. His trusteeship principle, namely that those who possess wealth must do so as trustees of the poor, was equally inconvenient to both camps and sounded, very odd at the time, as it does even today *prima facie*. Yet I wish thinkers of today go into this principle deeply. I have every hope that economic relations eventually will need to be redefined on the basis of a new meaning to be attached to the concepts of ownership and possession. The assertion that all land belongs to God is fully ingrained in Indian thought since time immemorial, and Gandhi's derives from it.

41. FRANKLIN D ROOSEVELT (1882–1945)

Franklin Delano Roosevelt, an American statesman, was the US president from 1933 (and the only man ever elected to four terms) till his death.

The following speech is his declaration of war on Japan, made on 8 December 1941.

*M*r Vice President, Mr Speaker, members of the Senate and the House of Representatives:

Yesterday, December 7, 1941 – a date which will live in infamy – the United States of America was suddenly and deliberately attacked by naval and air forces of the empire of Japan.

The United States was at peace with that nation, and, at the solicitation of Japan, was still in conversation with its government and its Emperor, looking toward the maintenance of peace in the Pacific. Indeed, one hour after Japanese air squadrons had commenced bombing in the American island of Oahu, the Japanese ambassador to the United States and his colleague delivered to our Secretary of State a formal reply to a recent American message. And, while this reply stated that it seemed useless to continue the existing diplomatic negotiations, it contained no threat or hint of war or of armed attack.

It will be recorded that the distance of Hawaii from Japan makes it obvious that the attack was deliberately planned many days or even weeks ago. During the intervening time, the Japanese Government has deliberately sought to deceive the United States by false statements and expressions of hope for continued peace.

The attack yesterday on the Hawaiian Islands has caused severe damage to American naval and military forces. I regret to tell you that very many American lives have been lost. In addition, American ships have been reported torpedoed on the high seas between San Francisco and Honolulu.

Yesterday, the Japanese Government also launched an attack against Malaya. Last night Japanese forces attacked Hong Kong. Last night Japanese forces attacked Guam. Last night Japanese forces attacked the Philippine Islands. Last night the Japanese attacked Wake Island. And this morning the Japanese attacked Midway Island. Japan has therefore undertaken a surprise offensive extending throughout the Pacific area. The facts of yesterday and today speak for themselves. The people of the United States have already formed their opinions and well-understand the implications to the very life and safety of our nation.

As commander-in-chief of the army and navy, I have directed that all measures be taken for our defense, that always will our whole nation remember the character of the onslaught against us. No matter how long it may take us to overcome this premeditated invasion, the American people, in their righteous might, will win through to absolute victory. I believe that I interpret the will of the Congress and of the people when I assert that we will not only defend ourselves to the uttermost but will make it very certain that this form of treachery shall never again endanger us.

Hostilities exist. There is no blinking at the fact that our people, our territory and our interests are in grave danger. With confidence in our armed forces, with the unbounding determination of our people, we will gain the inevitable triumph. So help us God. I ask that the Congress declare that since the unprovoked and dastardly attack by Japan on Sunday, December 7, 1941, a state of war has existed between the United States and the Japanese empire.

42. SOCRATES (470–399 BC)

Socrates was a Greek philosopher, Plato's master and an intellectual leader who attracted many followers.

He addressed a large gathering at Athens – after being charged with and found guilty of impiety and corrupting the young.

*I*n this space of time, O Athensians, you will incur the wrath and reproach at the hands of those who wish the defame the city Athens, of having put me the wise man, Socrates, to death. If those who wish to defame you had waited for a short time, this would have happened of its own accord; for observe my age, that it is far advanced in life, and near death. But I say this not to you all, but to those only who have condemned me to die. And I say this too to the same persons. Perhaps you think, O Athenians, that I have been convicted through the want of arguments, by which I might have persuaded you, had I thought it right to do and say anything so that I might escape punishment. For otherwise: I have been convicted through want indeed, yet not of arguments, but of audacity and impudence, and of the inclination to say such things to you as would have been most agreeable for you to hear, had I lamented and bewailed and done and said many other things unworthy of me, as I affirm, but such as you are accustomed to hear from others.

Neither did I then think that I ought for the sake of avoiding danger, to do anything unworthy of a freeman, nor do I now repent of having so defended myself; but I should much rather choose to die having so defended myself than to live in that way. For neither in a trial nor in battle is it right that I or any one else should employ every possible means whereby he may avoid death; for in battle it is frequently evident that a man might escape death by laying down his arms and throwing himself on the mercy of his pursuers. And there are many other devices in every danger, by which to avoid death, if a man dares to do and say everything.

But this is not difficult, O Athenians, to escape death, but it is much more difficult to avoid depravity, for it runs swifter than death. And now, being slow and aged, an overtaken by the slower of the two; but my accusers, being strong and active, have been overtaken by the swifter, wickedness. And now I depart, condemned by you to death; but they condemned by truth, as guilty of iniquity and injustice; and I abide by sentence and so do they. These things, perhaps, ought so to be, and I think that they are for the best.

In the next place, I desire to predict to *you* who have condemned me, what will be *your* fate: for I am now in that condition in which men most frequently prophesy, namely, when they are about to die. I say then to you, O Athenians, who have condemned me to death, that immediately after my death a punishment will overtake you, far more severe, by Jupiter, than that which you have inflicted on me, for you have done this thinking you should be freed from the necessity of giving an account of your life. The very contrary, however, as I affirm, will happen to you. Your accusers will be more numerous, whom I have now restrained, though you did not perceive it; and they will be more severe in as much as they are younger and will be more indignant. For, it you think that by putting me to death you will restrain anyone from upbraiding you because you do not live well, you are much mistaken, for this method of escape is neither possible nor honourable; but that offer is most honorable and most easy, not to put a check upon others, but for man to take heed to himself, how he may be most perfect. Having predicted thus, much to those of you who have condemned me, I take my leave of you.

But with you who have voted for my acquittal, I would hold converse on what has now taken place, while the magistrates are busy and I am not yet carried to the place where I must die. Stay with me then, so long, O Athenians, for nothing hinders our conversing with each other whilst we are permitted to do so, for I wish to make known to you, as being my friends, the meaning of that which has just now befallen me. To me then, O my judges, and in calling you judges I call you rightly, a strange thing has happened. For the wonted prophetic voice of my guardian deity, on every former occasion, even in the most trifling affairs, opposed me, if I was about to do anything wrong; but now, that has befallen me which you yourselves behold, and which anyone would think and which is supposed to be extremity of evil, yet neither when I departed from home in the morning did the warning of the god oppose me, nor when I came up here to the place of trial, nor in my address when I was about to say anything; yet on other occasions in has frequently restrained me in the midst of speaking. But now it has never throughout this proceeding opposed me, either in what I did or said. What then do I suppose to be the cause of this? I will tell you; what has befallen me appears to be a blessing; and it is impossible that we think rightly who suppose that death is an evil. A great proof of this to me is the fact that it is impossible but that the accustomed signal should have opposed me, unless I had been about to meet with some good.

Moreover, we may hence conclude that there is great hope that death is a blessing. For to die is one of two things: for either the dead may be annihilated and have no sensation of anything whatever; or as it is said, there is a change and a passage of the soul from one place to another. And if it is a privation of all sensation, as it were, a sleep in which the sleeper has no dream, death would be a wonderful gain. For I think that if anyone, having selected a night in which he slept so soundly as not to have had a dream, and having compared this night with all the other nights and days of his life, should be required on consideration to say how many days and nights he had passed better and more pleasantly than this night throughout his life, I think that not only a private person, but even a great king himself would find them easy to number in comparison with other days and nights. If, therefore, death is a thing of this kind, I say it is a gain; for thus all futurity appears to be nothing more than one night.

But if, one the other hand, death is a removal from hence to another place, and what is said to be true, that all the dead are there, what greater blessing can there be than this, my judges? For if, on arriving at Hades, released from these who pretend to be judges, one shall find those who are true judges and where said to judge there, Minos and Rhadamanthus, Aeacus and Triptolemus, and such others of the demigods as were just during their own life, would this be a sad removal? At what price would you estimate a conference with Orpheus and Musaes, Hesiod and Homer? I indeed should be willing to die often if this be true. For to me the sojourn there would be admirable, when I should meet with Palamedes, and Ajex, son of Telamon, and any other of the ancients who has died by an unjust sentence. The comparing my sufferings with theirs would, I think, be no unpleasing occupation. But the greatest pleasure would be to spend my time in questioning and examining the people there as I have done those here, and discovering who aiming them is wise, and who fancies himself to be so but is not. At what price, my judges, would not anyone estimate the opportunity of questioning him who led the mighty army against Troy, or Ulysses, or Sisyphus, or ten thousand others, whom one might mention, both men and women, with whom to converse and associate, and to question them, would be an inconceivable happiness. Surely for that the judges there do not condemn to death; for in other respects those who live there are more happy than those that are here, and are henceforth immortal, if at least what is said be true.

You therefore, O my judges, ought to entertain good hopes with respect to death, and to meditate on this one truth, that to a good man nothing is evil, neither while living nor when dead, nor are his concerns neglected by the gods. And what has befallen me is not the effect of chance; but his is clear to me, that now to die, and be free from my cares, is better for me. On this account the warning in no way turned me aside; and I bear no resentment towards those who condemned me, or against my accusers, although they did not condemn and accuse me with this intention, but thinking to injure me: in this they deserve to be blamed.

This much, however, I beg of them. Punish my sons, when they grow up, O judges, paining them as I have pained you, if they appear to you to care for the riches or anything else before virtue, and if they think themselves to be something when they are nothing, reproach them as I have done you, for not attending to what they ought, and for conceiving themselves something when they are worth nothing. If ye do this, both I and my sons shall have met with just treatment at your hands.

It is now time to depart, for me to die, for you to live. But which of us is going to a better state is unknown to everyone but God.

43. MOTHER TERESA (1910–1997)

Mother Teresa, the 'angel of mercy', founded the Missionaries of Charity in Kolkata, which set up about 570 homes for the poor and spread in about 125 countries, serving the poorest of the poor.

The following is the National Prayer Breakfast Speech by her in Washington D.C. on February 4, 1994.

On the last day, Jesus will say to those at his right hand, "Come, enter the Kingdom. For I was hungry and you gave me food, I was thirsty and you gave me drink, I was sick and you visited me."

Then Jesus will turn to those on his left hand and say,

"Depart from me because I was hungry and you did not feed me, I was thirsty and you did not give me drink, I was sick and you did not visit me."

These will ask him,

"When did we see you hungry, or thirsty, or sick, and did not come to your help?"

And Jesus will answer them,

"Whatever you neglected to do unto one of the least of these, you neglected to do unto me!"

As we have gathered here to pray together, I think it will be beautiful if we begin with a prayer that expresses very well what Jesus wants us to do for the least. St. Francis of Assisi understood very well these words of Jesus and his life is very well expressed by a prayer. And this prayer, which we say everyday after Holy Communion, always surprises me very much, because it is very fitting for each one of us. And I always wonder whether eight hundred years ago when St. Francis lived, they had the same difficulties that we have today. I think that some of you already have this prayer of peace, so we will pray it together.

Let us thank God for the opportunity he has given us today to have come here to pray together. We have come here especially to pray for peace, joy, and love. We are reminded that Jesus came to bring the good news to the poor. He had told us what that good news is when he said,

"My peace I leave with you, my peace I give unto you."

He came not to give the peace of the world, which is only that we don't bother each other. He came to give peace of heart which comes from loving—from doing good to others.

And God loved the world so much that he gave his son. God gave his son to the Virgin Mary, and what did she do with him? As soon as Jesus came into Mary's life, immediately she went in haste to give that good news. And as she came into the house of her cousin, Elizabeth, Scripture tells us that the unborn child—the child in the womb of Elizabeth—leapt with joy. While still in the womb of Mary, Jesus brought peace to John the Baptist, who leapt for joy in the womb of Elizabeth.

And as if that were not enough—as if it were not enough that God the Son should become one of us and bring peace and joy while still in the womb, Jesus also died on the Cross to show that greater love. He died for you and for me, and for that leper and for that man dying of hunger and that naked person lying in the street—not only of Calcutta, but of Africa, of everywhere. Our Sisters serve these poor people in 105 countries throughout the world. Jesus insisted that we love one another as he loves each one of us. Jesus gave his life to love us, and he tells us that he loves each one of us. Jesus gave his life to love us, and he tells us that we also have to give whatever it takes to do good to one another.

And in the Gospel, Jesus says very clearly, " Love as I have loved you."

Jesus died on the Cross because that is what it took for him to do good for us—to save us from our selfishness and sin. He gave up everything to do the Father's will, to show us that we too must be willing to give everything to do God's will, to love one another as he loves each of us. If we are not willing to give whatever it takes to do good for one another, sin is still in us. That is why we too must give to each other until it hurts.

Love always hurts.

It is not enough for us to say, "I love God." But I also have to love my neighbour. St. John says that you are a liar if you say you love God and you don't love your neighbour. How can you love God whom you do not see, if you do not love your neighbour whom you see, whom you touch, with whom you live? And so it is very important for us to realize that love, to be true, has to hurt. I must be willing to give whatever it takes not to harm other people and, in fact, to do good to them. This requires that I be willing to give until it hurts. Otherwise, there is no true love in me and I bring injustice, not peace, to those around me.

It hurt Jesus to love us. We have been created in his image for greater things, to love and to be loved. We must "put on Christ," as Scripture tells us. And so we have been created to love as he loves us. Jesus makes himself the hungry one, the naked one, the homeless one, the unwanted one, and he says, "You did it to me." On the last day he will say to those on his right, "whatever you did to the least of these, you did to me," and he will also say to those on his left, "whatever you neglected to do for the least of these, you neglected to do it for me."

When he was dying on the Cross, Jesus said, "I thirst." Jesus is thirsting for our love, and this is the thirst for everyone, poor and rich alike. We all thirst for the love of others, that they go out of their way to avoid harming us and to do good to us. This is the meaning of true love, to give until it hurts.

I can never forget the experience I had in visiting a home where they kept all these old parents of sons and daughters who had just put them into an institution and, maybe, forgotten them. I saw that in that home these old people had everything: good food, comfortable place, television—everything. But everyone was looking toward the door. And I did not see a single one with a smile on his face.

I turned to Sister and I asked, "Why do these people, who have every comfort here—why are they all looking toward the door? Why are they not smiling?" I am so used to seeing the smiles on our people. Even the dying ones smile. And Sister said, "This is the way it is, nearly everyday. They are expecting —they are hoping—that a son or daughter will come to visit them. They are hurt because they are forgotten."

See, this neglect to love brings spiritual poverty. Maybe in our family we have somebody who is feeling lonely, who is feeling sick, who is feeling worried. Are we there? Are we willing to give until it hurts, in order to be with our families? Or do we put our own interests first? These are the questions we must ask ourselves, especially as we begin this Year of the Family. We must remember that love begins at home, and we must also remember that the future of humanity passes through the family.

I was surprised in the West to see so many young boys and girls given to drugs. And I tried to find out why. Why is it like that, when those in the West have so many more things than those in the East? And the answer was, "Because there is no one in the family to receive them." Our children depend on us for everything: their health, their nutrition, their security, their coming to know and love God. For all of this, they look to us with trust, hope, and expectation. But often father and mother are so busy that they have no time for their children, or perhaps they are not even married, or have given up on their marriage. So the children go to the streets, and get involved in drugs, or other things. We are talking of love of the child, which is where love and peace must begin. These are the things that break peace.

But I feel that the greatest destroyer of peace today is abortion, because it is a war against the child—a direct killing of the innocent child—murder by the mother herself. And if we accept that a mother can kill even her own child, how can we tell other people not to kill one another? How do we persuade a woman not to have an abortion? As always, we must persuade her with love, and we remind ourselves that love means to be willing to give until it hurts. Jesus gave even his life to love us. So the mother who is thinking of abortion, should be helped to love— that is, to give until it hurts her plans, or her free time, to respect the life of her child. The father of that child, whoever he is, must also give until it hurts. By abortion, the mother does not learn to love, but kills even her own child to solve her problems. And by abortion, the father is told that he does not have to take any responsibility at all for the child he has brought into the world. That father is likely to put other women into the same trouble. So abortion just leads to more abortion. Any country that accepts abortion is not teaching the people to love, but to use any violence to get what they want. That is why the greatest destroyer of love and peace is abortion.

Many people are very, very concerned with the children of
India, with the children of Africa, where quite a few die of hunger,
and so on. Many people are also concerned about all the violence
in this great country of the United States. These concerns are
very good. But often these same people are not concerned with
the millions who are being killed by the deliberate decision of
their own mothers. And this is what is the greatest destroyer of
peace today: abortion, which brings people to such blindness.

"I want this child!"

And for this I appeal in India and I appeal everywhere: "Let
us bring the child back." The child is God's gift to the family.
Each child is created in the special image and likeness of God for
greater things — to love and to be loved. In this Year of the Family
we must bring the child back to the center of our care and concern.
This is the only way that our world can survive, because our
children are the only hope for the future. As other people are
called to God, only their children can take their places.

But what does God say to us? He says, "Even if a mother
could forget her child, I will not forget you. I have carved you in
the palm of my hand." We are carved in the palm of his hand;
that unborn child has been carved in the hand of God from
conception, and is called by God to love and to be loved, not only
now in this life, but forever. God can never forget us.

I will tell you something beautiful. We are fighting abortion
by adoption — by care of the mother and adoption for her baby.
We have saved thousands of lives. We have sent word to the
clinics, to the hospitals, and police stations: Please don't destroy
the child; we will take the child." So we always have someone
tell the mothers in trouble: "Come, we will take care of you, we
will get a home for your child."

And we have a tremendous demand from couples who cannot
have a child. But I never give a child to a couple who has done
something not to have a child. Jesus said, "Anyone who receives
a child in my name, receives me." By adopting a child, these
couples receive Jesus, but by aborting a child, a couple refuses to
receive Jesus.

Please don't kill the child. I want the child. Please give me the
child. I am willing to accept any child who would be aborted,
and to give that child to a married couple who will love the
child, and be loved by the child. From our children's home in

Calcutta alone, we have saved over 3,000 children from abortions. These children have brought such love and joy to their adopting parents, and have grown up so full of love and joy! I know that couples have to plan their family, and for that there is natural family planning. The way to plan the family is natural family planning, not contraception. In destroying the power of giving life, through contraception, a husband or wife is doing something to self. This turns the attention to self, and so it destroys the gift of love in him or her. In loving, the husband and wife must turn the attention to each other, as happens in natural family planning, and not to self, as happens in contraception. Once that living love is destroyed by contraception, abortion follows very easily.

The greatness of the poor.

I also know that there are great problems in the world – that many spouses do not love each other enough to practice natural family planning. We cannot solve all the problems in the world, but let us never bring in the worst problem of all, and that is to destroy love. This is what happens when we tell people to practice contraception and abortion.

The poor are very great people. They can teach us so many beautiful things. Once one of them came to thank us for teaching them natural family planning, and said: "You people – who have practiced chastity - you are the best people to teach us natural family planning, because it is nothing more than self-control out of love for each other." And what this poor person said is very true. These poor people maybe have nothing to eat, maybe they have not a home to live in, but they can still be great people when they are spiritually rich. Those who are materially poor can be wonderful people. One evening we went out and we picked up four people from the street. And one of them was in a most terrible condition. I told the Sisters: "You take care of the other three; I will take care of the one who looks worse." So I did for her all that my love can do. I put her in bed, and there was a beautiful smile on her face. She took hold of my hand, and she said one thing only: "Thank you." Then she died.

I could not help but examine my conscience before her. I asked, "What would I say if I were in her place?" And my answer was very simple. I would have tried to draw a little attention to myself. I would have said, "I am hungry, I am dying, I am cold, I am in pain," or something like that. But she gave me much more – she gave me her grateful love. And she died with a smile on her face.

Then there was the man we picked up from the drain, half-eaten by worms. And after we had brought him to the home, he only said, "I have lived like an animal in the street, but am going to die as an angel, loved and cared for." Then, after we had removed all the worms from this body, all he said—with a big smile—was: "Sister, I am going home to God." And he died. It was so wonderful to see the greatness of that man, who could speak like that without blaming anybody, without comparing anything. Like an angel, this is the greatness of people who are spiritually rich, even when they are materially poor.

A sign of care.

We are not social workers. We may be doing social work in the eyes of some people, but we must be contemplatives in the heart of the world. For we must bring that presence of God into your family, for the family that prays together, stays together. There is so much hatred, so much misery, and we with our prayer, with our sacrifice, are beginning at home. Love begins at home, and it is not how much we do, but how much love we put into what we do.

If we are contemplatives in the heart of the world with all its problems. These problems can never discourage us. We must always remember what God tells us in the Scripture: Even if the mother could forget the child in her womb—something that is impossible, but even if she could forget—I will never forget you. And so here I am talking with you. I want you to find the poor here, right in your own home first. And begin love there. Bear the good news to your own people first. And find out about your next-door neighbors. Do you know who they are?

I had the most extraordinary experience of love of a neighbour from a Hindu family. A gentleman came to our house and said, "Mother Teresa, there is a family who have not eaten for so long. Do something." So I took some rice and went there immediately. And I saw the children, their eyes shining with hunger. I don't know if you have ever seen hunger, but I have seen it very often. And the mother of the family took the rice I gave her, and went out. When she came back, I asked her, "Where did you go? What did you do?" And she gave me a very simple answer: "They are hungry also." What struck me was that she knew. And who were "they?" A Muslim family. And she knew. I didn't bring any more rice that evening, because I wanted them—Hindus and Muslims—to enjoy the joy of sharing.

But there were those children, radiating joy, sharing the joy and peace with their mother because she had the love to give until it hurts. And you see, this is where love begins: at home, in the family. God will never forget us, and there is something you and I can always do. We can keep the joy of loving Jesus in our hearts, and share that joy with all we come in contact with. Let us make that one point: that no child will be unwanted, unloved, uncared for, or killed and thrown away. And give until it hurts —with a smile.

Because I talk so much of giving with a smile, once a professor from the United States asked me, "Are you married?" And I said, "Yes, and I find it sometimes very difficult to smile at my spouse—Jesus—because he can be very demanding—sometimes this is really something true. And there is where love comes in— when it is demanding, and yet we can give it with joy.

One of the most demanding things for me is traveling everywhere, and with publicity. I have said to Jesus that if I don't go to heaven for anything else, I will be going to heaven for all the traveling with all the publicity, because it has purified me and sacrificed me and made me really ready to go to heaven. If we remember that God loves us, and that we can love others as he loves us, then America can become a sign of peace for the world. From here, a sign of care for the weakest of the weak— the unborn child—must go out to the world. If you become a burning light of justice and peace in the world, then really you will be true to what the founders of this country stood for. God bless you!

44. MARSHALL JOSIP BROZ TITO (1892–1990)

Marshall Tito became the first communist prime minister of modern Yugoslavia in 1945, and president in 1953.
The following speech was delivered against the German forces on 26 November 1942.

Comrades, brothers and sisters delegates of the Anti-Fascist Council of People's Liberation of Yogoslavia!

I welcome you on behalf of Supreme Headquarters, on behalf of the fighting men, commanders and political commissars of our heroic People's Liberation Army and Partisan Detachments of Yugoslavia.

I consider it great honour that the opportunity has offered itself for me to welcome you here today at this historic assembly, after the great and tough and bloody struggle which our people have had to wage during the past eighteen months.

I open this historic assembly of the anti-Fascist Council of People's Liberation of Yugoslavia, and I should now like to say a few words to you.

The result of the long, and bloody struggle – an unusual struggle, because we went into battle almost bare-handed – the result of this struggle is that today we have the opportunity to meet here, to create an instrument, a body which together with the Supreme Headquarters of the people's Liberation Army and Partisan Detachments of Yugoslavia, and together with the people's liberation committees, will be the backbone of our struggle; it will organise our devastated country economically and politically – in so far as such a thing can be done in the circumstances – in order that we may bring this bitter struggle to a victorious conclusion.

Comrades, we have no possibility of setting up a legal government, because international relations and conditions do not permit it as yet. But, comrades, we have a right to one thing, namely, we have the right in these critical circumstances to set up eg, a political body, a political instrument, to rally the people's masses, to rally our people and conduct them, together with out heroic army, into the new battles ahead of us—battles that will be exceedingly bitter. We have no authorities in our territory with the exception of our people's liberation committees which have been set up by the people themselves. We do not recognise the various fascist puppet government, and that is precisely why, here in this land, in our own land, soaked with the blood of the best sons of our people, we have to create conditions in which our people can—in such circumstances as the present—contribute their utmost to People's Liberation Struggle. While we were a small partisan army and had only small partisan detachments, the requirements were not great. Today those small partisan detachments have become a mighty People's Liberation Army which is not merely the equal of, but is superior to, the enemy in stamina and morale, in spite of the enemy's technical superiority. And so it is that the requirements are very much greater than before when every village, district, or community was able to feed its own fighting men. It is necessary to organise the authority, the political power, possessed by our people and to canalise it in one general direction—into the battle against the criminal fascist invaders, and against their allies, the traitors in our midst—the Ustashi, the Chetniks, and others.

I am happy to see here today the best sons of our people, patriots, true representatives of our people who have been steeled in this bitter and bloody struggle. They are no longer, as was once the case, representatives selected by canvassers. They are men who have grown in this superhuman struggle—out of the very heart of the people; men who have gone into battle prepared to lay down their lives. I am happy to see here today what is really the flower of our nation.

Comrades, a heavy burden, a great responsibility, falls upon our Anti-Fascist Council of People's Liberation of Yugoslavia. We possess, so to speak, nothing. We have only the weapons which we captured with the blood of our best fighting men. Our country is devastated, our people are enduring terrible sufferings and misery, hungry, naked, barefooted, exposed to the bestial terror of the Chetniks, the Ustashi, and the invader. But we have one thing—the unswerving firmness and faith of our afflicted people that victory will be theirs. Our morale is high, not only the morale of our army—which has astonished the whole world but also the morale of the people. Just look at the burnt-down villages. Nearby, in the freezing cold, in shacks or under the open sky, in the woods beside a fire, you can see peasants and their wives; but they do not bewail their fate, they say: Dear brothers, fight! We are prepared to give our last crust if it will help you to beat our common enemy. That is king of morale that is rarely seen—something that the Yugoslav peoples can be proud of.

It is only natural that the organism which we are creating here, which has grown up from below, should bear a heavy responsibility and have a huge task to fulfil. Our army needs weapons—and we have no arms factories. Our army needs food. All these things fall upon this great forum which our people have created as the nucleus of their authority. I think there is no one among you who is afraid of these hard tasks and great responsibilities. I think you are all prepared to sacrifice everything in the coming struggle which promises victory to our army. We have done battle and will continue to do with the enemy in spite of his superiority in arms. Hand-in-hand with you, comrades, who are the representatives of our peoples, our Supreme Headquarters will easily be able to surmount all the difficulties that lie ahead. Today we accept these difficulties, and overcome them, more easily than six months ago. Today the prospect is clear—its as clear as the sun that victory is on the side of the Allies. The Hitlerite and other fascist bands are today suffering from defeat after defeat. The heroic Red Army has been delivering deadly blows to the German fascist hordes and Hitler's satellites. Stalingrad, the fortress of the whole of progressive humanity, has been defended. Hundreds of thousands of German soldiers have perished in this and earlier offensives, beneath the walls of the city-of-flint. The Hitlerite fascists hurl themselves in every direction, like wild beasts in a cage; but there is no hope for them. In their death throes, they will perhaps try to wreck their rage upon the weaker, occupied countries, upon the occupied nations. But we can tell them that in Yugoslavia, they will have a really tough time. Today we have an army. Today we have arms—everything from rifles to field guns. We can measure up to them all right. You may rest assured that their power in our country is not sufficient to realise and put into effect their diabolical intentions, that is, to destroy us. We have never lost faith, and today least of all do we doubt that victory is ours. Consequently, at this moment, when the hearts of all subjugated peoples are beating with joy as they see the inevitable defeat of the fascist beasts, we go forward, boldly and full of hope and faith, to meet all the difficulties awaiting us, convinced that by working together and fighting, we shall carry our long struggle and our suffering to a triumphant close.

I wish you, the great national forum, the Anti-Fascist Council of People's Liberation of Yugoslavia, every success in your future work for the welfare of our peoples, for the welfare of our valiant People's Liberation Army, and in the interests of the unity of all the nationalities in Yugoslavia, for that is the foundation which is now being built, the foundation of brotherhood, unity, and concord, which no one will ever be able to destroy. This historic assembly is proof of the unity of our peoples—Serbs, Croats, S'ovenes, Mentenegrins, Muslims—and it is, at the same time, a guarantee that progress is being made in creating a better and happier future for our people.

45. HARRY S TRUMAN (1884–1972)

Harry Truman was the US president from 1945 to 1953. He was responsible for the decision to drop the first atom bomb.
This speech was delivered after the bombing of Hiroshima on 6 August 1945.

Sixteen hours ago, an American airplane dropped one bomb on Hiroshima, an important Japanese army base. That bomb had more power than 2,000 times the blast power of the British Grand Slam, which is the largest bomb ever yet used in the history of warfare.

The Japanese began the war from the air at Pearl Harbour. They have been repaid manifold. And the end is not yet. With this bomb we have now added a new and revolutionary increase in destruction to supplement the growing power of our armed forces. In their present form these bombs are now in production, and even more powerful forms are in development.

It is an atomic bomb. It is a harnessing of the basic power of the universe. The force from which the sun draws its power has been loosed against those who brought war to the Far East.

Before 1939, it was the accepted belief of scientists that it was theoretically possible to develop a practical method of doing it. By 1942, however, we knew that the Germans were working feverishly to find a way to add atomic energy to the other engines of war with which they hoped to enslave the world. But they failed. We may be grateful to Providence that the Germans got the V-1s and V-2s late and in limited quantities and more grateful that they did not get the atomic bomb at all.

The battle of the laboratories held fateful risks for us as well as the battles of the air, land, and sea, and we have now won the battle of the laboratories as we have won the other battles.

Beginning in 1940, before Pearl Harbour, scientific knowledge useful in war was pooled between the United States and Great Britain, and many priceless helps to our victories have come from that arrangement. Under that general policy, the research on the atomic bomb was begun. With American and British scientists working together, we entered the race of discovery against the Germans.

We are now prepared to obliterate more rapidly and completely every productive enterprise the Japanese have above ground in any city. We shall destroy their docks, their factories, and their communications. Let there be no mistake; we shall completely destroy Japan's power to make war.

It was to spare the Japanese people from utter destruction that the ultimatum of July 26 was issued at Potsdam. Japan's leaders promptly rejected that ultimatum. If they do not now accept our terms they may expect a rain of ruin from the air, the like of which has never been seen on this earth. Behind this air attack will follow sea and land forces in such numbers and power as they have not yet seen and with the fighting skill of which they are already well aware.

The Secretary of War, who has kept in personal touch with all phases of the project, will immediately make public a statement giving further details.

His statement will give facts concerning the sites at Oak Ridge near Knoxville, Tennessee, and at Richland near Pasco, Washington, and an installation near Santa Fe, New Mexico. Although the workers at the sites have been making materials to be used in producing the greatest destructive force in history, they have not themselves been in danger beyond that of many other occupations, for the utmost care has been taken of their safety.

The fact that we can release atomic energy ushers in a new era in man's understanding of nature's forces. Atomic energy may in the future supplement the power that now comes from coal, oil, and falling water, but at present it cannot be produced on a basis to compete with them commercially. Before that time comes, there must be a long period of intensive research.

It has never been the habit of the scientists of this country or the policy of this government to withhold from the world scientific knowledge. Normally, therefore, everything about the work with atomic energy would be made public.

But under present circumstances it is not intended to divulge the technical processes of production or all the military applications, pending further examination of possible methods of protecting us and the rest of the world from the danger of sudden destruction.

I shall recommend that the Congress of the United States consider promptly the establishment of an appropriate commission to control the production and use of atomic power within the United States. I shall give further consideration and make further recommendations to the Congress as to how atomic power can become a powerful and forceful influence towards the maintenance of world peace.

46. MARK TWAIN (1835–1910)

Mark Twain (pseudonym of Samuel Langhorne Clemens) was America's leading humorist who used his wit to comment on social, political and moral problems.

The following speech on right to vote for women was made by him on 20 January 1901.

*L*adies and Gentlemen: It is a small help that I can afford, but it is just such help that one can give as coming from the heart through the mouth. The report of Mr. Meyer was admirable, and I was as interested in it as you have been. Why, I'm twice as old as he, and I've had so much experience that I would say to him, when he makes his appeal for help: "Don't make it for today or tomorrow, but collect the money on the spot."

We are all creatures of sudden impulse. We must be worked up by steam, as it were. Get them to write their wills now, or it may be too late by-and-by. Fifteen or twenty years ago I had an experience I shall never forget. I got into a church which was crowded by a sweltering and panting multitude. The city missionary of our town—Hartford—made a telling appeal for help. He told of personal experiences among the poor in cellars and top lofts requiring instances of devotion and help. The poor are always good to the poor. When a person with his millions gives a hundred thousand dollars, it makes a great noise in the world, but he does not miss it; it's the widow's mite that makes no noise but does the best work.

I remember on that occasion in the Hartford church the collection was being taken up. The appeal had so stirred me that I could hardly wait for the hat or plate to come my way. I had four hundred dollars in my pocket, and I was anxious to drop it in the plate and wanted to borrow more. But the plate was so long in coming my way that the fever-heat of beneficence was going down lower and lower—going down at the rate of a hundred dollars a minute. The plate was passed too late. When it finally came to me, my enthusiasm had gone down so much that I kept my four hundred dollars—and stole a dime from the plate. So, you see, time sometimes leads to crime. Oh, many a time have I thought of that and regretted it, and I adjure you all to give while the fever is on you.

Referring to woman's sphere in life, I'll say that woman is always right. For twenty-five years I've been a woman's rights man. I have always believed, long before my mother died, that, with her gray hair and admirable intellect, perhaps she knew as much as I did. Perhaps she knew as much about voting as I.

I should like to see the time come when women shall help to make the laws. I should like to see that whiplash, the ballot, in the hands of women. As for this city's government, I don't want to say much, except that it is a shame—a shame; but if I should live twenty-five years longer—and there is no reason why I shouldn't—I think I'll see women handle the ballot. If women had the ballot today, the state of things in this town would not exist.

If all the women in this town had a vote today, they would elect a mayor at the next election, and they would, rise in their might and change the awful state of things now existing here.

47. ATAL BEHARI VAJPAYEE (1926–)

Vajpayee was the prime minister of India from 1998 to 2003. He is a social worker and a parliamentarian. He was actively involved in the nation's struggle for freedom.

He delivered this speech at the inauguration of the International Convention of the Global Organisation of People of Indian Origin, at New Delhi, on 6 January 2001.

*I*t gives me great pleasure to join you for the inauguration of this International Convention of Global Organisation of People of Indian Origin. Many of you have travelled great distances to attend this conference. In a sense, this is also a homecoming for you.

Today, there are nearly 20 million people of Indian origin living in almost every corner of the world. Rare is the country where you will not come across people of Indian origin. They have adopted foreign shores as their own. But neither the passage of time nor the distance between their ancestral land and their new homes has been able to sever the umbilical cord between Mother India and her children abroad.

You are as much the inheritors of India's rich civilisational heritage as your brothers and sisters back home in India. And, we are proud that you have kept alive your distinct cultural identity even while making a place for yourselves in a foreign social and cultural milieu.

We are equally proud of the fact that people of Indian origin, wherever they may be living, have greatly enriched the society, economy and culture of their adopted countries. The success stories of Indian entrepreneurs abroad are legendary. From hi-tech chip laboratories to curry restaurants, from renowned hospitals to famous educational institutions, from well-known research centres to leading think-tanks—everywhere you will find an Indian who has overcome all odds to establish himself through skill, dedication and hard work.

Your adopted countries have benefited from your unique contributions to their social and economic transformation. You have also contributed towards enhancing awareness about India's past history, present reality and future potential.

Indeed, from the sweat and tears of indentured Indian labour toiling on colonial sugar and tea plantations in the nineteenth century to the intellectual achievements of the Indian software community in the Silicon Valley of the twenty-first century, the odyssey of the Indian community at large is a reflection of the potential of our people and the magnitude of their contribution towards global prosperity.

Friends, I have often come across people of Indian origin who are eager to participate in India's nation-building efforts — as a tribute to the country of their origin, as a means of strengthening the bonds of love and affection that exists between them and India. The cooperation and valuable support extended by people of Indian origin and nonresident Indians during the last decade of economic liberalisation and structural reforms have greatly encouraged us and contributed to the birth of resurgent India.

Today, India stands on the threshold of a technological revolution in many areas that define the 'New Economy' of the twenty-first century; information technology, biotechnology, agriculture, space and energy.

Many of you owe your current success to the quality education which you have received in government run institutions, be they Indian Institutes of Technology or medical colleges. You now owe it to your motherland to associate yourself with India's search for rapid and enduring social change and economic progress.

I would like to emphasise that we do not merely seek investment and asset transfer. What we seek is a broader relationship — in fact, a partnership among all children of Mother India so that our country can emerge as a major global player. We value the role of people of Indian origin as unofficial ambassadors providing a link between India, and the rest of the world.

My government's policy is to assist the overseas Indian community in maintaining its cultural identity and strengthening the emotional, cultural and spiritual bonds that bind them to the country of their origin. With this objective in mind, we have constituted a high level committee on the Indian diaspora, headed by Shri L M Singhvi. This committee has been tasked to study the expectations of overseas Indians from India. It will study the role that people of Indian origin and nonresident Indians can play in the economic, social and technological progress of India. It will examine the current regime that governs your travel and stay in India as well as your investment in the Indian economy. It will recommend measures to resolve the problems faced by you.

More fundamentally, the committee has been asked to review the status of people of Indian origin and nonresident Indians in the context of the constitutional provisions, laws and rules applicable to them both in India and the countries of their residence.

Friends, the underpinnings of our civilisational history and cultural heritage have been the tradition of tolerance, openness to new ideas, respect for ancient wisdom, intellectual pursuit and abhorrence of violence. The people of Indian origin and nonresident Indians are a living testimony to the noble tradition of blending the old with the new.

With these words, I am pleased to inaugurate this International Convention of the Global Organisation of People of Indian Origin.

48. SWAMI VIVEKANANDA (1863–1902)

Swami Vivekananda (Narendranath) was a great Indian saint-philosopher. He made India's greatness known to the world, and established the Sri Ramakrishna Mission.

He gave the following welcome speech at the World Conference of Religions in Chicago on 11 September 1893.

Sisters and Brothers of America:
It fills my heart with joy unspeakable to rise in response to the warm and cordial welcome which you have given us. I thank you in the name of the most ancient order of monks in the world; I thank you in the name of the mother of religions, and I thank you in the name of millions and millions of Hindu people of all classes and sects.

My thanks, also, to some of the speakers on this platform who, referring to the delegates from the Orient, have told you that these men from far-off nations may well claim the honour of bearing to different lands the idea of toleration. I am proud to belong to a religion which has taught the world both tolerance and universal acceptance. We believe not only in universal toleration, but we accept all religions as true. I am proud to belong to a nation which has sheltered the persecuted and the refugees of all religions and all nations of the earth. I am proud to tell you that we have gathered in our bosom the purest remnant of the Israelites, who came to Southern India and took refuge with us in the very year in which their holy temple was shattered to pieces by Roman tyranny. I am proud to belong to the religion which has sheltered and is still fostering the remnant of the grand Zoroastrian nation. I will quote to you, brethren, a few lines from a hymn which I remember to have repeated from my earliest boyhood, which is everyday repeated by millions of human beings: "As the different streams having their sources in different paths which men take through different tendencies, various though they appear, crooked or straight, all lead to Thee."

The present convention, which is one of the most august assemblies ever held, is in itself a vindication, a declaration to the world of the wonderful doctrine preached in the Gita: "Whosoever comes to Me, through whatsoever form, I reach him; all men are struggling through paths which in the end lead to me." Sectarianism, bigotry, and its horrible descendant, fanaticism, have long possessed this beautiful earth. They have filled the earth with violence, drenched it often and often with human blood, destroyed civilization and sent whole nations to despair. Had it not been for these horrible demons, human society would be far more advanced than it is now. But their time is come; and I fervently hope that the bell that tolled this morning in honour of this convention may be the death-knell of all fanaticism, of all persecutions with the sword or with the pen, and of all uncharitable feelings between persons winding their way to the same goal, but through different ways.

The seed is put in the ground, and earth and air and water are placed around it. Does the seed become the earth, or the air, or the water? No. It becomes a plant. It develops after the law of its own growth, assimilates the air, the earth, and the water, converts them into plant substance, and grows into a plant.

Similar is the case with religion. The Christian is not to become a Hindu or a Buddhist, nor a Hindu or a Buddhist to become a Christian. But each must assimilate the spirit of the others and yet preserve his individuality and grow according to his own law of growth.

If the Parliament of Religions has shown anything to the world, it is this: It has proved to the world that holiness, purity and charity are not the exclusive possessions of any church in the world, and that every system has produced men and women of the most exalted character. In the face of this evidence, if anybody dreams of the exclusive survival of his own religion and the destruction of the others, I pity him from the bottom of my heart, and point out to him that upon the banner of every religion will soon be written, in spite of resistance: "Help and not fight", "Assimilation and not Destruction", "Harmony and Peace and not Dissension".

49. GEORGE WASHINGTON (1732–1799)

George Washington was the first president of the US.
The following is the inaugural address to the Congress on
30 April 1789.

*A*mong the vicissitudes incident to life no event could have filled me with greater anxieties than that of which the notification was transmitted by your order, and received on the 14th day of the present month. On the one hand, I was summoned by my country, whose voice I can never hear but with veneration and love, from a retreat which I had chosen with the fondest predilection, and, in my flattering hopes with an immutable decision, as the asylum of my declining years—a retreat which was rendered everyday more necessary as well as more dear to me by the addition of habit to inclination, and of frequent interruptions in my health to the gradual waste committed on it by time. On the other hand, the magnitude and difficulty of the trust to which the voice of my country called me, being sufficient to awaken in the wisest and most experienced of her citizens a distrustful scrutiny into his qualifications, could not but overwhelm with despondence one who, inheriting inferior endowments from nature and unpractised in the duties of civil administration, ought to be peculiarly conscious of his own deficiencies. In this conflict of emotions, all I dare ever is that it has been my faithful study to collect my duty from a just appreciation of every circumstance by which it might be affected. All I dare hope is that if, in executing this task, I have been too much swayed by a grateful remembrances of former instances, or by an affectionate sensibility to this transcendent proof of the confidence of my fellow citizens, and gave thence too little consulted my incapacity as well as disinclination for the weighty and untried cares before me, my error will be palliated by the motives which mislead me, and its consequences be judged by my country with some share of the partiality in which they originated.

Such being the impressions under which I have, in obedience to the public summons, repaired to the present station, it would be peculiarly improper to omit in this first official act my fervent supplications to that Almighty Being who rules over the universe, who presides in the councils of nations, and whose providential aids can supply every human defect, that His benediction may consecrate to the liberties and happiness of the people of the United States and the government instituted by themselves for these essential purposes, and may enable every instrument employed in its administration to execute with success the functions allotted to this charge. In tendering this homage to the Great Author of every public and private good, I assure myself that it expresses your sentiments not less than my own, nor those of my fellow citizens at large less than either. No people can be bound to acknowledge and adore the Invisible Hand which they have advanced to the character of an independent nation seems to have been distinguished by some token of providential agency; and in the important revolution just accomplished in the system of their united government the tranquil deliberations from which the event has resulted cannot be compared with the means by which most governments have been established without some return of pious gratitude, along with an humble anticipation of the future blessings which the past seem to presage. These reflections, arising out of the present crises, have forced themselves too strongly on my mind to be suppressed. You will join with me, I trust, in thinking that there are none under the influence of which the proceedings of a new and free government can more auspiciously commence.

By the article establishing the executive department, it is made the duty of the president to recommend to your consideration such measures as he shall judge necessary and expedient. The circumstances under which I now meet you will acquit me from entering into that subject further than to refer to the great constitutional charter under which you are assembled, and which, in defining your powers, designates the objects to which your attention is to be given. It will be more consistent with those circumstances, and far more congenial with the feelings which actuate me, to substitute, in place of a recommendation of particular measures, the tribute that is due to the talents, the rectitude, and the patriotism which adorn the characters selected to devise and adopt them. In these honourable qualifications I behold the surest pledges that as on one side on local prejudices or attachments, no separate views nor party animosities, will misdirect the comprehensive and equal eye which ought to watch over this great assemblage of communities and interests, so, on another, that the foundation of our national policy will be laid in the pure and immutable principles of private morality, and the preeminence of free government be exemplified by all the attributes which can win the affections of its citizens and command the respect of the world. I dwell on this prospect with every satisfaction which an ardent love for my country can inspire, since there is no truth more thoroughly established than that there exists in the economy and course of nature an indissoluble union between virtue and happiness; between duty and advantage; between the genuine maxims of an honest and magnanimous policy and the solid rewards of public prosperity and felicity; since we ought to be no less persuaded that the propitious smiles of Heaven can never be expected on a nation that disregards the eternal rules of order and right which Heaven itself has ordained; and since the preservation of the sacred fire of liberty and the destiny of the republican model of government are justly considered, perhaps, as deeply, as finally, staked of the experiment intrusted to the hands of the American people.

Besides the ordinary objects submitted to your care, it will remain with your judgement to decide how far an exercise of the occasional power delegated by the fifth article of the Constitution is rendered expedient at the present juncture by the nature of objections which have been urged against the system, or by the degree of inquietude which has given birth to them. Instead of undertaking particular recommendations on this subject, in which I could be guided by no lights derived from official opportunities, I shall again give way to my entire confidence in your discernment and pursuit of the public good; for I assure myself that whilst you carefully avoid every alteration which might endanger the benefits of a united and effective government, or which ought to await the future lessons of experience, a reverence for the characteristic rights of freemen and a regard for the public harmony will sufficiently influence your deliberations on the question how far the former can be impregnably fortified or the latter be safely and advantageously promoted.

To the foregoing observations I have one to add, which will be most properly addressed to the House of Representatives. It concerns myself, and will therefore be as brief as possible. When I was first honoured with a call into the service of my country, then on the eve of an arduous struggle for its liberties, the light in which I contemplated my duty required that I should renounce every pecuniary compensation. From this resolution I have in no instance departed; and being still under the impressions which produced it, I must decline as inapplicable to myself any share in the personal emoluments which may be indispensably included in a permanent provision for the executive department, and must accordingly pray that the pecuniary estimates for the station in which I am placed may during my continuance in it be limited to such actual expenditures as the public good may be thought to require.

Having thus imparted to you my sentiments as they have been awakened by the occasion which brings us together, I shall take my present leave; but not without resorting once more to the benign Parent of the Human Race in humble supplication that, since He has been pleased to favour the American people with opportunities for deliberating in perfect tranquillity and perfect dispositions for deciding with unparalleled unanimity on a form of government for the security of their Union and the advancement of their happiness, so His divine blessing may be equally conspicuous in the enlarged views, the temperate consultations, and wise measures on which the success of this government must depend.

50. WOODROW WILSON (1856–1924)

Woodrow Wilson was the US president from 1913 to 1921.

He appeared before a joint session of Congress on January 8, 1918 and made this 14-point address, suggesting possible peace terms to end the four-year-old conflict. Soldiers from England, France, Germany, Russia and many other nations had died by the millions.

Gentlemen of the Congress:

*O*nce more, as repeatedly before, the spokesmen of the Central Empires have indicated their desire to discuss the objects of the war and the possible basis of a general peace. Parleys have been in progress at Brest-Litovsk between Russian representatives and representatives of the Central Powers to which the attention of all the belligerents has been invited for the purpose of ascertaining whether it may be possible to extend these parleys into a general conference with regard to terms of peace and settlement.

The Russian representatives presented not only a perfectly definite statement of the principles upon which they would be willing to conclude peace, but also an equally definite programme of the concrete application of those principles. The representatives of the Central Powers, on their part, presented an outline of settlement which, if much less definite, seemed susceptible of liberal interpretation until their specific programme of practical terms was added. That programme proposed no concessions at all, either to the sovereignty of Russia or to the preferences of the populations with whose fortunes it dealt, but meant, in a word, that the Central Empires were to keep every foot of territory their armed forces had occupied—every province, every city, every point of vantage as a permanent addition to their territories and their power.

The Russian representatives have insisted, very justly, very wisely, and in the true spirit of modern democracy, that the conferences they have been holding with the Teutonic and Turkish statesmen should be held within open, not closed, doors, and all the world has been audience, as was desired.

But whatever the results of the parleys at Brest-Litovsk, whatever the confusions of counsel and of purpose in the utterances of the spokesmen of the Central Empires, they have again attempted to acquaint the world with their objects in the war and have again challenged their adversaries to say what their objects are and what sort of settlement they would deem just and satisfactory. There is no good reason why that challenge should not be responded to, and responded to with the utmost candor. Within the last week Mr. Lloyd George has spoken with admirable candor and in admirable spirit for the people and government of Great Britain.

There is no confusion of counsel among the adversaries of the central powers, no uncertainty of principle, no vagueness of detail. The only secrecy of counsel, the only lack of fearless frankness, the only failure to make definite statement of the objects of the war, lies with Germany and her allies. The issues of life and death hang upon these definitions.

We entered this war because violations of right had occurred which touched us to the quick and made the life of our own people impossible unless they were corrected and the world secured once for all against their recurrence.

What we demand in this war, therefore, is nothing peculiar to ourselves. It is that the world be made fit and safe to live in; and particularly that it be made safe for every peace-loving nation which, like our own, wishes to live its own life, determine its own institutions, be assured of justice and fair dealing by the other peoples of the world, as against force and selfish aggression.

All the peoples of the world are in effect partners in this interest, and for our own part we see very clearly that unless justice be done to others it will not be done to us.

The programme of the world's peace, therefore, is our programme; and that programme, the only possible programme, as we see it, is this:

1. Open covenants of peace must be arrived at, after which there will surely be no private international action or rulings

of any kind, but diplomacy shall proceed always frankly and in the public view.

2. Absolute freedom of navigation upon the seas, outside territorial waters, alike in peace and in war, except as the seas may be closed in whole or in part by international action for the enforcement of international covenants.

3. The removal, so far as possible, of all economic barriers and the establishment of an equality of trade conditions among all the nations consenting to the peace and associating themselves for its maintenance.

4. Adequate guarantees given and taken that national armaments will be reduced to the lowest points consistent with domestic safety.

5. A free, open-minded, and absolutely impartial adjustment of all colonial claims, based upon a strict observance of the principle that in determining all such questions of sovereignty the interests of the population concerned must have equal weight with the equitable claims of the government whose title is to be determined.

6. The evacuation of all Russian territory and such a settlement of all questions affecting Russia as will secure the best and freest cooperation of the other nations of the world in obtaining for her an unhampered and unembarrassed opportunity for the independent determination of her own political development and national policy, and assure her of a sincere welcome into the society of free nations under institutions of her own choosing; and, more than a welcome, assistance also of every kind that she may need and may herself desire.

7. Belgium, the whole world will agree, must be evacuated and restored, without any attempt to limit the sovereignty which she enjoys in common with all other free nations.

8. All French territory should be freed and the invaded portions restored, and the wrong done to France by Prussia in 1871 in the matter of Alsace-Lorraine, which has unsettled the peace of the world for nearly fifty years, should be righted, in order that peace may once more be made secure in the interest of all.

9. A readjustment of the frontiers of Italy should be effected along clearly recognizable lines of nationality.

10. The peoples of Austria-Hungary, whose place among the nations we wish to see safeguarded and assured, should be accorded the freest opportunity of autonomous development.
11. Romania, Serbia, and Montenegro should be evacuated; occupied territories restored; Serbia accorded free and secure access to the sea; and the relations of the several Balkan states to one another determined by friendly counsel along historically established lines of allegiance and nationality; and international guarantees of the political and economic independence and territorial integrity of the several Balkan states should be entered into.
12. The Turkish portions of the present Ottoman Empire should be assured a secure sovereignty, but the other nationalities which are now under Turkish rule should be assured an undoubted security of life and an absolutely unmolested opportunity of autonomous development, and the Dardanelles should be permanently opened as a free passage to the ships and commerce of all nations under international guarantees.
13. An independent Polish state should be erected which should include the territories inhabited by indisputably Polish populations, which should be assured a free and secure access to the sea, and whose political and economic independence and territorial integrity should be guaranteed by international covenant.
14. A general association of nations must be formed under specific covenants for the purpose of affording mutual guarantees of political independence and territorial integrity to great and small states alike.

In regard to these essential rectifications of wrong and assertions of right, we feel ourselves to be intimate partners of all the governments and peoples associated together against the imperialists. We cannot be separated in interest or divided in purpose. We stand together until the end.

We have spoken now, surely, in terms too concrete to admit of any further doubt or question. An evident principle runs through the whole programme I have outlined. It is the principle of justice to all peoples and nationalities, and their right to live on equal terms of liberty and safety with one another, whether they be strong or weak.

Unless this principle be made its foundation, no part of the structure of international justice can stand. The people of the United States could act upon no other principle, and to the vindication of this principle they are ready to devote their lives, their honour, and everything that they possess. The moral climax of this, the culminating and final war for human liberty has come, and they are ready to put their own strength, their own highest purpose, their own integrity and devotion to the test.